FROM BARTER TO BITCOIN
THE CRAZY EVOLUTION OF MONEY

JOHN HOFMEYR

First published by John Hofmeyr, 2021

Copyright © 2021 by John Hofmeyr

ISBN 978-0-620-91468-0 (print)

ISBN 978-0-620-92870-0 (e-book)

Editor: Phillipa Mitchell

(www.phillipamitchell.com)

Proofreader: Kelly-May Macdonald

(http://writeupyouralley.co.za/)

Cover design & Typesetting by Gregg Davies Media

(www.greggdavies.com)

All rights reserved

The moral right of the author has been asserted.

No part of this publication may be reproduced, distributed, or transmitted in any form or by any means, including photocopying, recording, or other electronic or mechanical methods, without the prior written permission of the author, except in the case of brief quotations embodied in critical reviews and certain other non-commercial uses permitted by copyright law.

Additional copies of this book can be purchased
from all leading book retailers worldwide.

Table of Contents

CAST OF CHARACTERS v

CHAPTER SYNOPSIS vii

PREFACE xi

EDEL LAWNE xiii

CHAPTER 1: NOTHING FOR NOTHING 1

CHAPTER 2: ...AND VERY LITTLE FOR SIXPENCE 13

CHAPTER 3: A STORE OF VALUE 19

CHAPTER 4: A PROMISE IS A PROMISE 37

CHAPTER 5: THE COLOUR OF YOUR MONEY 45

CHAPTER 6: THE VALUE OF TIME 55

CHAPTER 7: RICH MAN, POOR MAN – WHAT IS WEALTH? .. 69

CHAPTER 8: ...BEGGARMAN, THIEF 83

CHAPTER 9: SMART MONEY 101

CHAPTER 10: FUTURE-PROOFING 107

CHAPTER 11: WHAT'S TO BECOME OF ME? 125

GLOSSARY OF TERMS 131

TABLE OF FIGURES 147

About the Author: 155

CAST OF CHARACTERS

- **Jennie Stockitt** is the narrator – a fifteen-year-old girl living in the real world of this work of fiction (oxymoron intended). She chats to readers and connects the chapters through a series of dreams about the historical development of commercial matters. Jennie doesn't hold the stage for very long, though — she backs off, watches, listens and learns, as we do, chapter by chapter. All text relating to Jennie and the real world appears in blue.

- **Drennie Stockitt** is Jennie's *alter-ego*, also known as "Dream-Jennie". In Jennie's dreams, Drennie is the protagonist. Since she never does more work than is absolutely necessary, she is good at inventing new and better ways of completing her tasks – and generally achieving satisfactory outcomes. Drennie is smart and popular and can't resist ice-cream.

- **Mercy Stockitt** is Drennie's Mom. She is a merchant – the quintessential trader, general dealer and retailer who provides anything and everything the people need. She keeps a large inventory of all sorts of commodities that she buys in bulk at wholesale prices and then supplies to people who want only small quantities for themselves and their families.

- **"Scoop" Cooper** is a worker employed by Mercy Stockitt. He is good at making and selling ice-cream.

- **"Duckie" Planter** has green fingers. She is a wholesale dealer in foodstuffs, cultivates crops and vegetables, and keeps chickens and dairy cows. She is also a super caterer – her packed, take-away meals are popular.

- **"Strike" Klopper** is the blacksmith. He is skilled in making anything from metal. In the absence of a police force, he also fulfils the role of law enforcer.

- **Georgie Ford** is one of two antagonists in the book. He believes there's a sucker born every minute. He is thoroughly dishonest — the archetypal crook.

- **Claude Treacher** is Georgie Ford's co-antagonist. He's a dashing young jeweller and skilled goldsmith, but he's easily led, notably by Georgie Ford. Drennie develops a crush on him.

- **"Buzz" Sawyer** is a forester, woodworker and builder.

CHAPTER SYNOPSIS

1. NOTHING FOR NOTHING ...

We explore the concept of trade – exchanging one type of value for another. The concept of bartering is introduced, showing how trade is possible without using money. We also consider how the worth of the work (or goods) is valued. The advantage of specialisation is presented, and the inefficiencies of barter are highlighted.

2. ... AND VERY LITTLE FOR SIXPENCE

This brief chapter introduces efficiency and smart work as ways of adding value, instead of working harder (or longer) hours.

3. A STORE OF VALUE

Exchanging goods and services for other goods and services can be problematic because the needs of the traders must match at the same time. What if there was a way to overcome this problem by using a token of value to be provided later? And what about cheating?

4. A PROMISE IS A PROMISE

We introduce the concept of a simple promissory note as an alternative to the simultaneous exchange of goods. Its advantages include the ability to delay the requiting of a debt, and the ability to trade pieces of paper. The idea of bargaining is introduced, showing a way to establish fair value. Simple notes like these have their shortcomings. And what about forgery?

5. THE COLOUR OF YOUR MONEY

"Show me the colour of your money!" is a gambler's challenge to an opponent to prove that there is enough cash to pay if the bet is lost. But in this chapter, the phrase is used in its literal sense – the appearance of paper money. We introduce the standardisation of promise-notes leading to notes that were originally issued by private banks and later by countries' central banks. Descriptions follow about the concept of a deposit of fungible value (usually silver or gold), against which a note was issued and against which the silver or gold could be redeemed. We then consider the abandonment of this requirement and the evolution of 'fiat money'. This cements the concept of paying with banknotes (issued by a central bank) as we know them today.

6. THE VALUE OF TIME

The value of time is introduced by demonstrating that the value of goods (measured in money) varies from time to time and that having cash available immediately (or almost immediately) allows leverage.

7. RICH-MAN, POOR-MAN – WHAT IS WEALTH?

Much has been written and spoken about 'the poor' and 'the rich'. We explore the word 'wealth' and derive a definition based on 'value', as referred to in Chapter 5.

8. ...BEGGAR-MAN, THIEF

This chapter deals with dishonesty, thievery, fraud (and the like) of which we should beware. If it sounds too good to be true, it probably is. And what if too many tokens of value are chasing limited real value?

9. SMART MONEY

The term 'smart money' usually refers to intelligent investing in assets that increase in value, but in this chapter, we use the literal meaning of the phrase, touching on blockchain technology, cryptocurrencies like Bitcoin, and 'smart contracts'.

10. FUTURE-PROOFING

Previous chapters looked backwards to historical events. In this chapter, we speculate about the wondrous challenges of the future, including some educational requirements for participation in the twenty-first century's economies.

11. WHAT'S TO BECOME OF ME?

Jennie looks to her future by applying the lessons she has learned under Drennie's guidance. Will it be a career in entrepreneurship? Perhaps professional consulting? Or might it be teaching? Jennie also discovers a really good reason to get out of bed each morning.

PREFACE

"I should never have worried that I didn't know what I was talking about. Economics is an entire scientific discipline of not knowing what you're talking about."

P.J. O'Rourke – *Eat the Rich: A Treatise on Economics*

In this book, we light-heartedly explore many of the facets of commerce – money, value, worth, wealth, trade, and other related matters. We examine supply and demand, inflation, opportunity cost and trade-offs. While the primary thread of the story is commerce, it is also a 'general education' tool. Teachings include language, history and finance, as well as life lessons about fraud, financial scams and dishonesty. And since no book is complete without a love story, there is even a brief interlude of an unrequited teenage crush.

Experts may be distressed (and the target readership delighted) to see that there is not a single graph, nor chart, nor table in this book.

If readers find that they are not yet familiar with a term used in our stories, they are encouraged to use a dictionary or the internet to find its meaning before reading on. Some of them may be explained in the Glossary of Terms at the end of this book. Have a look there first.

EDEL LAWNE

Before the introduction of decimal currency in 1971, money was a complicated thing in the United Kingdom and its colonies. The British currency system was comprised of pounds, shillings and pennies (pence). A pound consisted of twenty shillings, and a shilling was comprised of twelve pence. In the 1960s, a week's pocket money for a middle-class child was a silver coin called a sixpence, as referred to in the next sentence and in the title of Chapter 2.

In the village of Edel Lawne, the people acknowledged with reverence the eighteenth-century British maxim, "*Nothing for nothing, and very little for sixpence.*"

Paraphrasing this, one may say, "*We live by the principle of exchanging value for value.*"

The opposite is also true – *"Cheating and stealing are easy, but disastrous when you get caught."*

The name of the village is an anagram of a well-known three-word phrase. Its middle word has two letters. Unravel the anagram to discover what the townsfolk really meant when they said, "W*e have EDEL LAWNE.*"[1]

---

1 See the Glossary of Terms if you can't work it out.

CHAPTER 1

NOTHING FOR NOTHING

My report card showed decent marks in most of my subjects, but I scored poorly in economics – again. As usual, my teacher's comments included the dreaded phrases, "Can do better" and "Must try harder".

Don't you hate it when teachers write that?

One evening, as I was preparing for bed, I reconsidered the research I had done for my assignment:

Discuss barter as a mechanism for exchanging value (500 words)

I remembered my teacher's advice: "Don't memorise and regurgitate the facts, Jennie. Try to think yourself into the matter. Experience the situations and imagine the logical consequences." So it was not altogether surprising that, as I drifted off to sleep that night, I found myself in an ancient village. Right away, I recognised myself as my alter-ego, Dream-Jennie, or Drennie for short.

Some people call it an allowance, others call it pocket money, but whatever you call it, Drennie Stockitt didn't get any of it. Just like teenagers all over the world, Drennie did her chores every day – well, sort of. Sometimes, in the heat of summer, her laziness would get the better of her and she would shirk her more strenuous duties.

The reason for the absence of pocket money was simple – during those ancient days in the village of Edel Lawne, there was no money at all.

- The people lived in beautiful homes built of fine, straight logs. But they had no money.

- They ate delicious soups, fresh bread and roast chicken, as well as potatoes and vegetables, pizza and ice-cream[2]. But they had no money.

- They had wonderful furniture, soft, warm beds, and the most comfortable rocking chairs. But they had no money.

---

2   Ice cream in the days of barter? Yes, but it was a rare and expensive delicacy. This is a dream, remember. Cut the author some slack! If you want to learn more about the history of ice-cream, visit https://www.idfa.org/the-history-of-ice-cream.

- The children's playground was fitted with swings and jungle-gyms made of timber and smoothed to a silky finish. Drennie and her friends never got splinters when they played there as youngsters. But the people had no money.

- Most importantly (from Drennie's viewpoint), she could get an ice-cream whenever she wanted one – well almost always – even though she (just like everybody else) had no money.

Were these villagers of Edel Lawne very poor? How did they have all those wonderful symbols of wealth without having any money? It was quite simple, really – the townsfolk worked together to make things as simple as possible. Everybody was good at something, so each person did the things that they could do expertly and quickly. Without any arrogance, they would say, "*I should do that because I can do it more efficiently than you.*"

The villagers had one unbreakable rule:

EXCHANGE VALUE FOR VALUE

While it may seem that they did what they did for nothing, something was always owed in return.

Drennie's mom, Mercy Stockitt, ran the town's store. It was a super-general dealer where the townsfolk could get just about anything. She called herself "Mercy-the-Merchant".

Mercy worked closely with Duckie Planter who dealt in *everything* to do with food, mostly on a wholesale basis. Duckie planted and harvested crops, raised livestock, and ran the dairy. She also cooked the best meals in town. Duckie's enterprise was called FARM 'n KITCHEN.

Duckie was also living evidence that you should never trust a thin chef.

Duckie knew how important it was that the villagers stayed healthy, so she was fastidious about cleanliness and hygiene. All her harvesting and food-making equipment was washed down daily with a potent disinfectant. Keeping the milk urns germ-free was the worst. Scrupulously cleaning and sanitising them was just the beginning. After they were scrubbed clean and disinfected, Duckie would place the urns in a large tub and rinse them with boiling water, heated in a wood-fired furnace. If she didn't rinse them properly, the milk would take on a rather strange taste. It was a critically important job, but boy, was it laborious.

One day, Buzz Sawyer, the carpenter, savoured the aromas wafting through the air from Duckie's kitchen as he approached. He and his three sons were going to spend the next day chopping down trees, so they needed some food to take with them.

"Duckie," he said, "please make a picnic lunch for the boys and me for tomorrow. We'll be in the woods all day. And please include something to drink – we'll be far from the stream."

"Sure, I'll do that," smiled Duckie. "Four lunch-packs as usual?"

"Yes, please," said Buzz.

"They'll be ready for you at 7 a.m.," she said.

Just as Buzz was about to turn around and leave, Duckie remembered something.

"Buzz," she said, "my roof needs some work – the rain dripped onto my bed during last night's storm. I didn't sleep a wink. When can you repair it for me?"

"I have time right now," said Buzz, "I'll do it right away."

So:

- Nobody asked for a favour.
- Nobody did anything for nothing.
- Buzz and his woodchopper sons got their lunch.
- Duckie got her roof fixed.
- Nobody used any money.

But most importantly:

- Duckie and Buzz were both satisfied with the value of the trade.

I half-awoke from my dream, feeling a bit of a disconnect about it all. While I recognised that Duckie and Buzz's trade made sense back then, I wondered what would have happened if Duckie had wanted to rebuild her house. That would be worth a heck of a lot of sandwiches! Imagine wanting an ice-cream and then spending an hour figuring out what to give the ice-cream supplier in return.

Before I drifted off to sleep again, I remembered an image I had found online that I was planning to use in my assignment.

Figure i

A woodcut from *Historia de gentibus septentrionalibus* (History of the Nordic peoples), by Olaus Magnus, dated 1555.

Goods traded included implements (axes, knives and scissors), weaponry (bows and arrows) and foodstuffs.

No money changed hands.

Part of Mercy Stockitt's regular trade with FARM 'n KITCHEN included the daily delivery of several large urns full of fresh milk from Duckie Planter. Mercy would decant the milk into bottles so that the townsfolk could get one or two bottles of milk at a time. According to Duckie's hygiene protocol, the urns and bottles had to be washed out and disinfected before they could be used again. This job was Drennie's most detested manual chore. It involved over an hour of hard labour, lugging the empty urns and bottles about, washing, rinsing and disinfecting them, then carefully rinsing everything again so that the disinfectant residue didn't curdle the milk or make it taste odd.

As Drennie grew up, she began to understand a bit more about how the world worked in Edel Lawne. Getting an ice-cream whenever she wanted one troubled her a little. She knew that nobody else got anything for nothing in Edel Lawne, but "Scoop" Cooper (the man who worked for Mercy-the-Merchant and made ice-cream) always gave her a cone when she asked for one and never required anything from her in return.

"Well, he works for my Mom," Drennie mused. "Maybe that's why."

She barely noticed Scoop making a note in the little book he kept in his pocket afterwards.

One stinking hot day, Drennie's heart leapt when she heard Scoop's ice-cream bell tinkling in the distance. There he was, riding down the road towards her with his tantalising icebox attached to his tricycle. Feeling lazy – as she often did in the warm summer months – she waited in the shade of a tree until he got close enough for her to hail him.

"Hi!" she called out as he approached. "It must be jolly hot, pedalling and peddling like that." Drennie giggled at her own homophonic pun.

"It's a perfect day for an ice-cream," she continued. "Please give me a double-scoop, Scoop."

The ice-cream man smiled at her play on words and at her (recurring) joke about his nickname. Drennie licked her lips in anticipation.

"Hmm," he responded. "Let me see now."

Drennie watched as Scoop took his little book from his pocket. She noticed his furrowed brow as he studied his notes.

"Nope," he said, eventually.

"Whaddayamean *'Nope'*?" Drennie cried, somewhat discourteously. "It's the hottest day of the year! I need an ice-cream before I melt."

"It's not complicated," said Scoop quietly, almost as if he had rehearsed the conversation. "Nope means nope. It's a colloquial term for 'No'. And I'll thank you to mind your tone of voice when you address me, young lady."

"Sorry, Scoop – I didn't mean to be rude," said Drennie. "But what's wrong? I guess that it's such a hot day that you must be sold out?"

"No fear," laughed Scoop, "I saw the weather forecast, so I made lots last night. There's plenty of ice-cream in here."

Scoop tapped the icebox, gave her his biggest smile and made off down the street, tinkling his bell.

"But none for *you* today," he said to himself, when he was far enough away for Drennie not to hear him.

After he rounded the next corner, Drennie couldn't see him changing his route and heading straight for Mercy's store. And, of course, she didn't overhear their conversation, which ended with "... *exactly as you predicted, Mercy.*"

Drennie was acutely aware that Scoop worked for her mother. While she thought about taking her complaint to Mercy, there was a niggling voice in the back of her head that told her not to make a fuss. Surprisingly, the matter came up for conversation during dinner that evening – and the way it happened made Drennie blush from her hairline to her boots.

Mercy mentioned that she had given Scoop some extra time off because he'd worked late the previous evening, making extra ice-cream in preparation for the hot weather.

"So you're on ice-cream duty tomorrow, Drennie," she added.

Drennie contemplated – with much distaste – the morrow's hours of gently stirring the freezing mixture, keeping it creamy, and not allowing the ice crystals to get large and crunchy. That was nearly as detestable a chore as washing milk bottles and urns – but at least it was cool in the ice-cream room.

"I would have loved an ice-cream today, Mom," Drennie lamented. "The heat was fierce, but Scoop wouldn't give me one."

"I know, dear," said her mother, almost too kindly. "You might have noticed that I had to clean out the milk urns and bottles this morning ..." The unfinished sentence hung over the dinner table like the Cheshire Cat's grin.[3]

Seeing Drennie blush, Mercy knew that her daughter acknowledged the consequence of failing to perform her

---

[3] If you recognised this devious reference, well done. If you didn't, visit the Glossary of Terms at the end of this book.

task of cleaning the milk containers. Drennie had learned her lesson the hard way.

I awoke right away, annoyed that Drennie hadn't realised the purpose of Scoop's notebook. I know that cursing is unacceptable, but I reckoned it would be okay … just as long as I didn't say it out loud.

"Damn!" I thought. "Why couldn't Drennie see what was happening?" Mercy and Scoop were balancing the performance of Drennie's chores against the provision of ice-cream, and everything had been recorded in Scoop's little notebook. It was a record of *value provided* against *value received*. When Scoop gave Drennie an ice-cream, it *wasn't* something-for-nothing after all – it was an exchange of value for value.

CHAPTER 2

...AND VERY LITTLE FOR SIXPENCE

In a recent history class, we studied the ancient Greek myth of Sisyphus. One day, Death arrived to take Sisyphus, but he decided to cheat the system, chaining Death up so that he would not be taken. Even though he was not successful in his underhanded scheme, Sisyphus had another trick up his sleeve, and was sent back from the underworld to live out the rest of his life. The god Zeus was so angry with Sisyphus for his trickery that when he died a second time, Zeus condemned him to roll a huge rock up a hill in Hades for all of eternity. As punishment, each time Sisyphus approached the summit, he would lose control of the boulder. It would roll down the hill, and Sisyphus would have to start rolling it up the hill again. And again. And again.

As I drifted off to sleep, I immediately recognised Drennie when she appeared, but I barely recognised the town. It had undergone significant development. The townsfolk had even installed a hydroelectric generator, powered by water from a dam they'd built across the river that flowed not far from the village of Edel Lawne.

Drennie was washing out the milk urns before returning them to Duckie Planter at FARM 'n KITCHEN. There were thousands of them. The more she washed, the more appeared. It seemed endless – just like poor Sisyphus and his rock. Two thoughts (each quite similar to the other) went around and around and around in Drennie's head as she washed away:

- If there is no advantage or disadvantage to anybody, is there any value attached to work that is done – or left undone?

- If an outcome is the same – whether a task is completed or not – what is the value of the completed task?

I sat bolt upright in my bed, the image of Drennie glowing in my mind's eye. Every urn that she meticulously washed, scrubbed, disinfected and rinsed was about to go straight into Duckie Planter's washing-disinfecting-rinsing-boiling procedure. What a waste of Drennie's time!

"*Hmm...,*" I thought. "*What should Drennie do about this inefficiency?*"

I promptly went back to sleep and continued my dream.

Drennie was fully aware that no one person in Edel Lawne worked harder than anyone else, nor did anyone work longer hours – but they certainly worked *smart*. That's why they achieved more. The value of something was measured only by its benefit to its receiver. No consideration was given to the amount of time, effort, skill and experience applied by the person who performed the tasks or supplied the goods. By the same token, inefficiency was never rewarded. People who struggled to achieve only minor outcomes soon abandoned their efforts and focused their energies on things they could do well – the things that truly *added* value.

With electricity now available in Edel Lawne, Duckie Planter invested in new equipment for FARM 'n KITCHEN – a powerful machine to wash and disinfect multiple milk urns and milk bottles at the same time, extremely efficiently, and at a high temperature. As it reached the end of its washing cycle, the machine blasted the bottles and urns with high-pressure steam to eliminate any remaining micro-organisms. In the final step, the machine printed a Certificate of Guarantee to accompany that batch of bottles and urns, confirming that they were disinfected and safe to use.

Duckie called it her LactoBactoBuster[4].

Suddenly, it all made sense. Drennie's manual washing and disinfecting of the urns before returning them, while extremely courteous, added no value because it came with no guarantee – which meant that Duckie would have to machine-wash the urns anyway.

---

4   "Lacto-": to do with milk. "Bacto-": to do with micro-organisms. "Buster" is urban slang, meaning to destroy something.

"I wonder how I can turn this inefficiency to my advantage?" mused Drennie.

A few days after Scoop's refusal to provide her with ice-cream, Drennie made an announcement over dinner.

"I've got a job, Mom – I'll be operating Duckie's LactoBactoBuster for an hour and a half every afternoon."

"What a good idea," said Mercy. "Did Duckie offer anything in return?"

"Yep! I got two benefits," Drennie replied. "The LactoBactoBuster has one setting for urns and another for bottles. I'll be taking the used urns *and our used bottles* to be cleaned in Duckie's machine. When I bring our bottles back, they'll be *certified* clean before you refill them with milk the next day."

"And the other benefit?" Mercy asked.

"Duckie will also deliver an extra five litres of cream to your store every day so that Scoop can make more ice-cream. And for every extra five litres of cream he gets, Scoop said I could have two litres of ice-cream, all for myself."

Seeing the horror written instantly all over Mercy's face, Drennie burst out laughing.

"Don't be silly, Mom," said Drennie. "I'm not going to eat all that ice-cream myself. Scoop will let me trade it for other things that I want."

She already had her eye on a new dress with quite a low-cut bodice. It was the dress her mother wouldn't get for her because it was *"inappropriate for a fifteen-year-old"*.

"Well, that's a relief," sighed Mercy.

"There are benefits all round, Mom," said Drennie. "To start with, Duckie's time will be freed up to do other work because I'll be operating her LactoBactoBuster. That's worth more to her than five extra litres of cream. Scoop can make an additional five litres of ice-cream, and he only has to give me two of them. That's worth three litres of ice-cream, at no cost to him. That compensates him for the ice-cream sales I make that he would have otherwise made. I get two litres of ice-cream to trade for other stuff – which is worth more to me than an hour and a half of work at Duckie's machine. And finally, you get certified-clean bottles without lifting a finger!"

Mercy could barely conceal her pride in her daughter's ingenuity and adherence to the principle of nothing for nothing.

CHAPTER 3

A STORE OF VALUE

The shortcomings of barter were clear to me. Surely something could be done ... but what, exactly? I did not have to wonder for very long for a dream to answer that question.

Drennie's ice-cream trading business was flourishing. She developed a keen understanding of the complexities of bartering – the simple swapping of one value for another. Often, people wanted an ice-cream but couldn't give Drennie what she wanted. She thought about the new dress with the low-cut bodice. That was worth many, many ice-creams.

"C'mon, brain," said Drennie to herself. "Think logically. How can one create a store of value so that the trading partners don't have to swap value for value simultaneously?"

Eventually, Drennie worked out a three-step process:

STEP 1

Identify something small and easy to carry, but difficult to find or to make. That will make it rare and difficult to copy which, in turn, makes it a token of value.

STEP 2

If these tokens have the same weight, size and shape, make them all the same worth. For Drennie, one month's manual labour (or the equivalent) would be an appropriate value.

STEP 3

Persuade the people that these tokens could be exchanged for goods or services to be provided in the future. Similarly, the tokens could be used as a reward for goods or services that had already been provided – for example, work that had already been completed.

Drennie suddenly thought of the gold nuggets that the townsfolk occasionally found in the river bed near to Edel Lawne. She knew that gold was rare, that it didn't rust like iron, and that it could be moulded or stamped into any shape – the perfect metal to use to make a token, an artificial nugget. If the idea was accepted, the townsfolk would eagerly pan for nuggets and gold dust in the nearby rivers and streams.

Drennie broached the subject that evening: "Mom," she said, "Do you think the townsfolk would like a way to simplify barter when the traders' wares don't match?"

"Perhaps," said Mercy. "Do you have an idea?"

Drennie described her idea of artificial golden nuggets, all the same size and shape, and all having the same value. Mercy saw its potential right away.

"Let's discuss this with Duckie," she suggested.

Duckie loved the idea, so the three of them went to ask Strike Klopper, the town's blacksmith, how the tokens could be made. Strike, too, loved the idea and said that he could make the tokens quite easily.

Right then and there, the idea of coins was born in Edel Lawne. The people knew a good idea when they saw one – and it wasn't long before everyone was using the little gold coin that they called the "Edel". Every Edel was indeed equivalent to the rate of pay for one month's unskilled work.

Some people made a full-time living from panning for gold in the rivers. These prospectors brought their gold dust and nuggets into town where, in full view of anybody who was interested, the shiny pieces of metal were weighed and converted into 'Edels'. Strike Klopper prepared the perfectly round moulds, heated the gold and bashed the coins out very efficiently. The gold was much softer and easier to melt than the iron he usually worked with. The townsfolk of Edel Lawne made a rule that anyone could witness the coin-making procedure – that way, there could be no cheating.

As a reward for making the gold Edels, Strike kept one-tenth of one percent of the gold that was brought to him. As we know by now, the townsfolk got nothing for nothing.

Panning in the rivers and streams for gold dust and nuggets was a bit of a hit-and-miss affair. If it wasn't profitable, it was unrewarding, back-breaking work.

The townsfolk found it strange to see Georgie Ford, an occasional visitor to Edel Lawne, standing ankle-deep in the river, bent over with a pan in his hand. Georgie never did an honest day's work if he could possibly avoid it. Interestingly, he always had an Edel or two, yet he never seemed to find much gold. Nor did he seem to do much work around the town.

If the villagers wondered where his coins came from, they paid it little heed. Drennie did, though. But she couldn't work it out.

Drennie applied the philosophy of storing value and, bit by bit, her savings increased. Since the low-cut dress was a luxury, she decided not to buy it right away – even though she had saved up enough Edels. And so, as time went on, her savings continued to increase. One day, she decided the time had come for her to buy her dress.

Imagine her delight when she arrived at the store to find a one-day special offer – three dresses for the price of two. She had saved up enough Edels to exploit that offer. She could hardly believe her luck – from saving up to buy one beautiful dress, she was now able to buy three!

Drennie never forgot the advantage of having extra savings available, either to take care of an emergency or to exploit a bonanza like the three dresses in the store.

HISTORICAL INTEREST BOX

Figure ii

The "Lydian Lion", arguably the world's oldest human-made coin, dates back to about 2600 years ago – even though it is reported that the Chinese were using bronze emulations of cowrie shells three hundred years earlier.[5] The Lydian Lion was made in modern-day Turkey from gold or a gold-silver alloy called Electrum. It was a bit like a gold nugget. While its widest dimension was typically about 15mm (a bit more than half an inch), it was usually about 4mm (one-sixth of an inch) thick. Some were as tiny as 3mm in diameter. Some show a lion and a bull, while others show only a lion. The value of one Lydian Lion could vary widely, depending on its size and the proportions of the precious metals of which it was

---

5 Ancient Chinese Cowry Shell, Relics of Chicago, http://www.relicsofchicago.com/ancient-chinese-cowry-shell.html.

comprised. Various historical exchanges for one Lydian Lion have been reported and include: one month's wage; three jars of wine; ten goats; or any number of sheep, ranging from as little as one to as many as eleven.

Figure iii

Cowrie seashells were accepted as a form of payment in large parts of Asia, Africa, Oceania, and some parts of Europe. They share certain characteristics with coins – they are somewhat rare, easily recognisable, durable, and convenient to carry. As they were transported further and further from the coast, so their rarity and value increased.

Figure iv　　　　　　　　Figure v

Both the Ghanaian 1-Cedi coin (left) and the early Chinese carved pieces of bone (right) indicate the cowrie shell as historical forms of money. Note the holes in the carved bone, for easy stringing. Since anybody could make such a carved item, its worth was based on trusting that the token would retain its value.

Figure vi

This is an ancient Roman coin called an "Aureus". ("Aurum" is the Latin word for gold.) As coins became more common, they became less like nuggets and more like the discs which we know today. Before the engravings are stamped, the disc is known as a "blank". In historical times, the blank was often not struck exactly in the middle, so the coins looked distinctly handmade and a bit unprofessional.

Drennie saw right away that, as beautiful as the golden Edels were, they were unsuitable for day-to-day buying and selling. Since an Edel was equivalent to one month's work, the people needed coins with a smaller denomination for smaller transactions. So, the villagers arranged for Strike Klopper to make simpler coins for smaller transactions. These were called:

- "dec" for one one-tenth of an Edel – these were made of silver alloy

- "cent" for one one-hundredth of an Edel – these were made of copper

- "mil" for one one-thousandth of an Edel – these were made of aluminium

- "tenk" for one ten-thousandth (ten-k) of an Edel – these were made of steel

Drennie thought that she might burst with pride when she saw the outcome of her idea. She knew the exact shape, thickness, weight, size and colour of every coin.

She was equally chuffed about their names, especially the "tenk" since it could be written as "ten-k" (meaning ten-thousand) – in other words, one ten-thousandth of an Edel. This would be the denomination used for buying low-value items like hamburgers, which would cost about twenty tenks. One scoop of ice cream would cost three or four tenks.

Almost immediately, a problem arose in Edel Lawne. The people noticed that golden Edels were getting thinner and thinner as the months went by, presumably from repeated handling. Fortunately, Strike Klopper knew about metals, and he quickly solved that problem by alloying the gold with a little copper to make it more durable. Anyone who so desired was allowed to watch as Strike carefully weighed the yellow gold and the red copper and prepared the alloy with exactly the right quantities of each metal. The copper gave the Edels an attractive red-gold colour.

It wasn't long before a far more serious problem became evident. Drennie noticed that the coins seemed to be reducing, not only in thickness but also in diameter.

"That can't be caused by abrasion from general usage," she said to herself. "Something else is happening."

Since she was the one who had invented the idea of the Edels, she made it her business to solve the puzzle.

"I'll just follow the money," she muttered under her breath.[6]

"Duckie," said Drennie one afternoon while she was operating the LactoBactoBuster, "please do me a favour. Next time Georgie Ford comes past to ask you to employ him for a month, please pay him with a brand new golden Edel."

"Okay," said Duckie. "I can do that – but why?"

"Just a hunch," said the young wannabe sleuth. "Maybe it's nothing. I don't want to embarrass myself – or you – if I'm wrong."

Not too long after that, Georgie was knocking at Duckie's door, asking for a job. Duckie agreed to give him one, and when Drennie arrived later that afternoon to disinfect the urns and the bottles, Duckie gave Drennie a gigantic wink, to remind her that she had not forgotten her earlier request.

As soon as Drennie had finished sterilising the urns and bottles, she went straight home.

"Mom," she said, "sometime next month, Georgie Ford will come to buy some stuff. He'll pay with a brand new Edel. Please put the coin aside for me to look at."

---

6   "Follow the money" is a phrase that investigators still use to this day when probing cases of fraud and corruption in business and government.

"Okay," said Mercy, " I can do that – but why?"

"Just a hunch," said Drennie. "Maybe it's nothing. I don't want to embarrass myself or you if I'm wrong."

It all unfolded precisely as Drennie had expected. Early the following month, she studied the Edel that Georgie Ford had made payment with earlier that day. What had started out as a brand new, perfectly round Edel now had a thin piece missing from around its edge. Georgie had shaved[7] a sliver of gold from the precious golden coin! Drennie was furious. He was damaging *her* Edels. She took it as a personal insult.

"Drennie, how on earth did you work out what Georgie was doing?" Mercy asked, after Drennie related her findings.

"Simple deduction," said Drennie proudly, trying hard not to sound like one of her teachers. "There are two types of gold in Edel Lawne – one is the freshly-panned yellow gold, and the *other* is the copper-alloyed Edel. I looked at the pieces of gold that Georgie brought to Strike. Some were panned gold, but most of the pieces were reddish. He was giving Strike the slivers he'd shaved from the alloyed coins and presenting the pieces as panned gold,

---

7 When no attempt is made to disguise the removal of a section of a coin, the procedure is called 'coin clipping'. For examples of this, visit https://www.britishmuseum.org/collection/object/C_1913-1204-205 and see Figure vii.

after he had roughed them up a bit."

It wasn't long before the whole town knew what Georgie had been up to. They were all just as mad as Drennie, and they gathered together in the village square to deal with him. Fortunately for Georgie – or perhaps thanks to his swindling lifestyle – he was a fast runner. He sprinted down the main street, chased by half the townsfolk, led by Strike Klopper who was brandishing a glowing steel rod.

"Good riddance!" they shouted as Georgie passed the outskirts of the town.

Drennie calculated that there was no way "Georgie Fraud" had been responsible for *all* the golden Edels that had been shaved down. There were most certainly other culprits involved. Soon, everybody in town became a suspect. Drennie decided that instead of challenging everybody to find the guilty parties, she was simply going to embarrass them. She watched the faces of the villagers as she explained her thoughts about Georgie having had some accomplices. The guilty ones were those whose faces glowed a bright shade of red when she mused, "I wonder who else was shaving the edges off the Edels?"

Georgie reappeared in Edel Lawne some days later, hungry, humble and forlorn. The gentle and merciful townsfolk accepted him back, much to Drennie's dismay. It wasn't long before he was up to further trickery.

The rest is history. Eventually, people stopped making their own tokens of value. They appointed government-controlled mints to manufacture their coins, which could be used in every town and city, no matter where in a country that town or city was. As time went on, coins no longer contained valuable metals – they were simply accepted as symbols or tokens of value that could be exchanged. These new coins solved the problem of dishonest folk shaving pieces from around the edges. To this day, coins only have value because people trust that value to be correct. The same is true of banknotes, as you will see in Chapter 5.

HISTORICAL INTEREST BOX

Figure vii

This is a gold coin called a solidus. Note how pieces have been shaved or clipped off the edges.

Figure viii

The problem of coin shaving was solved when coins were minted mechanically, and the idea of "reeding" took hold. Grooves – called "reeds" – were carved (or milled) into the edges of coins so that any evidence of tampering was immediately visible. Reeding also allowed people to identify different coins by touch alone. Coins of a low-denomination seldom go through the reeding process. Since they are made from base metals, they are not worth shaving.

CHAPTER 4

A PROMISE IS A PROMISE

While I admired the concepts of trust, honour, and value-for-value, what would happen if trust was broken in Edel Lawne? Thoughts of cheating and duplicity swirled around my mind, and it wasn't long before I was submerged in a dream.

One day, Duckie Planter needed a kilogram of seeds to grow vegetables, so she headed off to fetch some from Mercy-the-Merchant. Mercy happened to be out of town that day and had left Drennie in charge of the store.

Duckie offered Drennie ten chickens as an exchange of value.

"No, thanks," said Drennie. "Mom has enough chickens for now."

"Won't she need more in a few days?" Duckie asked.

"More like in a week," Drennie smiled.

"Okay," said Duckie, "I'll bring them next week."

Before Drennie handed over the seeds – and just so that nobody would forget – she prepared a promise-note for Duckie to sign that read as follows.

**I, Duckie Planter, promise to give to Mercy Stockitt:
TEN CHICKENS**

Duckie signed the note, gave it back to Drennie, and went off to plant her seeds.

The following day, while Duckie was carefully planting her seeds in the field behind FARM 'n KITCHEN, Mercy rushed over to her.

"Duckie, it's an EMERGENCY! I forgot that I have to make mashed potatoes for the school-kids' lunch tomorrow – and there are one-hundred-and-sixty of them! Can you supply me with forty kilograms of potatoes right away? Don't bother to wash them."

"I can," said Duckie, shaking the soil from her hands. "What are you offering?"

"How about four chickens?" Mercy suggested. "I've brought along Drennie's *TEN CHICKENS* note. How about we just change it? You can owe me six chickens instead of ten."

Duckie gave the suggestion some thought. "Four chickens would normally be a fair trade for forty kilograms of unwashed potatoes, Mercy, but right now I'm busy planting. For me to stop what I'm doing and dig up all those potatoes for you, you must reduce what I owe by more than four chickens."

"Okay," said Mercy, "How about five?"

"Agreed!" said Duckie.

They changed the promise-note to look like this:

I, Duckie Planter, promise to give to Mercy Stockitt:
FIVE ~~TEN~~ CHICKENS

And so, in that moment, the **TEN-CHICKEN-NOTE** disappeared and the **FIVE-CHICKEN-NOTE** was born.

EARLY HEADS-UP:

Reader, we will revisit this transaction in a later chapter. In the meantime, think about what changed the value of Mercy and Duckie's trade from six chickens to five.

Now, remember, the people of Edel Lawne thrive on efficiency, and one good idea often leads to a better one.

"Mercy," said Duckie, "my time is limited at the moment, but I'll have lots of free time available tomorrow morning. Since I'm a way better cook than you, why don't I make the mashed potatoes for you just before lunch-time? That way, you can deliver the food, still hot and ready to be dished up?"

"That's a great idea!" said a delighted Mercy. "Please do that."

With that, she promptly tore up the five-chicken-note.

"Now you owe me nothing, Duckie – but I'll owe you. You'll need more seeds in a few weeks. Can we trade the mashed potatoes for your next batch of seeds?"

"Could I get half a kilo of seeds then?" Duckie asked.

"It's a deal," said Mercy. She promptly wrote out a new note, almost identical to Drennie's, signed it, and handed it to Duckie.

> **I, Mercy Stockitt, promise to give to Duckie Planter:**
> **HALF A KILOGRAM OF VEGETABLE SEEDS**

The people of Edel Lawne soon learned about the **TEN-CHICKEN-NOTE** that became a **FIVE-CHICKEN-NOTE** – and eventually disappeared altogether. It wasn't long before they started using similar notes when there was a mismatch between what was needed and what was offered in return.

Soon after, they realised that stating the beneficiary's name restricted the usefulness of the note. So, when somebody needed something and didn't have any of their own goods on them at that moment, they simply wrote a note promising to provide those goods to the person who owned the promise-note (the "bearer").

Authentication was based on a simple signature, and looked a bit like this:

> **I, Duckie Planter, promise to give to Bearer:**
> **TWO KILOGRAMS OF ONIONS**
> *D. Planter*

Soon, promise-notes were going back and forth but, with changes often needing to be made, many of them began to look really messy. Mercy was struggling the most because she held inventory of just about everything people needed. Since she would exchange anything for anything at fair value, she did more trading than anyone else, and she wrote and received the largest number of promise-notes. So many, in fact, that she often found it difficult to remember having written a specific promise-note when it was presented to her weeks or even months later.

While both Duckie and Mercy were concerned that this might create an opportunity for forgery, they were too busy to do anything about it. Drennie was continuously suspicious of Georgie Ford, the coin-shaver, but couldn't keep an eye on him all day every day.

Late one afternoon, just before Mercy closed her store – and when it was most busy – Georgie brought her one of her promise-notes.

I, Mercy Stockit, promise to give to Bearer:
FIVE LITRES OF MILK

"Mercy, your promise-note says five litres of milk," the lazy ne'er-do-well scoundrel said, "but I need only two.

Please give me two litres, and change the note to say three."

"Where did you get this?" asked Mercy, squinting at the note.

"Strike Klopper gave it to me. He got it from you a few weeks ago, and I did some work for him yesterday."

Georgie began to feel uncomfortable.

"Drennie!" called Mercy. "Please ask Strike to come here. And tell him to bring a red-hot iron with him."

"What's wrong, Mercy?" cried the bewildered Georgie.

"Georgie Fraud, I'll have you know that on my promise-notes, I really DO ... KNOW ... HOW ... TO ... SPELL ... MY ... OWN ... NAME!"

Mercy's voice, rising in pitch and volume with each word, could be heard all over Edel Lawne.

"Your name should be GEORGIE FRAUD AND FORGER!" she hissed at him venomously.

Mercy wanted to run him out of town in the same way as the villagers had done when Drennie had caught him shaving the edges off the golden Edels. But the citizens of Edel Lawne were kindly, forgiving people. They allowed him to stay on one condition – he had to stop cheating, perform honest work, and live by their principle of exchanging value for value.

But Drennie was plagued with misgivings – could Georgie Fraud *really* ever mend his ways?

CHAPTER 5

THE COLOUR OF YOUR MONEY

My next dream was significantly more complicated than my previous visions. I recalled that while Drennie was minding her mom's store, she had invented the idea of the promise-note. I also remembered how messy the promise-notes had started to look as the townsfolk made changes to them. There had to be a way of simplifying things. As I began to doze off, I wondered what Drennie might do.

Drennie was trying to provide some ice-cream to an uncooperative buyer who wouldn't specify the quantity he wanted and just kept repeating, "Gimme ice-cream for the FULL VALUE of the note!" The promise-note had been changed repeatedly – it had several people's names on it and different quantities for a whole range of items. Mercy had promised vegetable seeds. Buzz Sawyer had promised sawn timber and roof-shingles. Strike Klopper had promised horse-shoes and lengths of wire. And it was all on the same note. What a disaster!

Drennie studied the messily-written promise-note, trying to decipher what the final promise was so that she knew how much ice-cream she could supply against it. Just as she thought she had figured it out, the accursed note changed into golden Edels, which slipped through her fingers.

(Don't you just hate it when this kind of thing happens in a dream?)

As the golden coins hit the floor, they didn't scatter like dropped marbles, but turned back into the unintelligible promise-note. When Drennie picked it up, the names and quantities of the different types of merchandise swirled and swayed into a mess of letters and numbers.

"Aaaaargh! Here we go again!" thought Drennie.

One by one, the letters and numbers disappeared until only seven characters were left. Drennie spelt the word out:

O-I-L-S-E-E-D

"OILSEED". Now *that* was surely the most useless promise-note that Drennie had ever seen. Not only was there no quantity, but there was no indication of where this mysterious *oilseed* could be obtained. In the meantime, the mysterious (and stubborn) ice-cream buyer had disappeared.

That OILSEED conundrum caused me to awaken. The image was so vibrant in my mind that I decided to use an old trick for remembering dreams:

WRITE IT DOWN AND THEN GO BACK TO SLEEP!

When I awoke the next morning, I had completely forgotten my dream until I saw the piece of notepaper on the desk next to my bed. I read what I had written down:

01 LSEED

That's when I remembered my dream. While Drennie had seen the seven letters that made up the word "OILSEED", I now saw a mixture of both numbers and letters: a "0" (zero), followed by a "1" (one), followed by a gap, and then the letters "L", "S", "E", "E" and "D". While it made no sense to me at all, I knew that a dream later that night would bring me clarity.

Drennie was wrestling with the meaning of *"01 LSEED"*. Suddenly, an idea struck her like a bolt of lightning. Since the promise-note was a jumble of letters and numbers, perhaps all she needed to do was jumble them all up again to make a new word or phrase.

Drennie jumbled and re-jumbled the seven alphanumerics, writing them down in one order after another. It was a bit like solving an anagram for a crossword puzzle.

Without turning the page, try to work out what the promise-note meant.

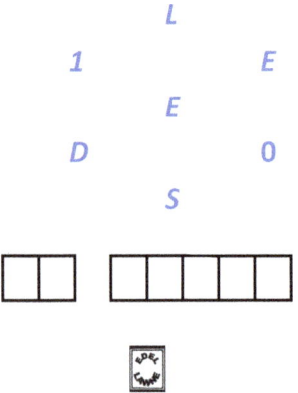

Then Drennie separated the numbers from the letters. Her eyes grew wide as she looked down at the promise-note in front of her:

10 EDELS

It all made sense now. That's why the complicated promise-note had turned into a handful of coins and then back again into a simplified (albeit rather cryptic) promise-note. It was trying to tell her that a promise-note could be a store of value for both goods (like chickens), *and* tokens of value (like coins).

"A token of a token," Drennie mused. Without a second's hesitation, she made her first experimental money-promise-note, which stated this: *I, Drennie Stockitt, promise to provide value to the extent of 10 EDELS.*

After she signed it, she giggled at the thought of providing a quantity of ice-cream equal to ten months' worth of wages. The mysterious buyer would be eating truckloads of it for months on end! So she made a second money-promise-note for '*1 EDEL*'. "That's more sensible," she thought.

Then she made a series of promise-notes equivalent to the fractional Edels. The experimental promise-notes showed 'One dec', 'One cent', 'One mil' and 'One tenk', each with the same value as the respective silver, copper, aluminium and steel coins which bore the same names.

Reader, try to work out why the very low-value notes (mils and tenks) turned out to be rather useless? Hint: it's the same reason why, to this day, we use coins for small transactions and banknotes for larger ones.

These money-promise-notes in Drennie's world were much like today's banknotes – a piece of paper that replaced the valuable silver or gold, which was the "real token" of value that was held in the bank's vault. Money-promise-notes, in turn, led to the creation of what we know today as banks, which took on the role of taking deposits and lending out money.

THE COLOUR OF YOUR MONEY | 51

HISTORICAL INTEREST BOX

Note the appearance of the certificates of deposit and the federal reserve note that were in use about one hundred years ago. They are similar to modern banknotes. The silver and gold certificates were exchangeable for silver or gold coins, while the Federal Reserve Note (the third image below) could only be exchanged for other dollar notes or coins equal to the value of the note, depending on what was in circulation at the time.

The statements on the notes have a rather disjointed phraseology. For ease of reference, they are reproduced below each note in uppercase.

Figure ix

"THIS CERTIFIES THAT THERE HAS BEEN DEPOSITED IN THE TREASURY OF THE UNITED STATES OF AMERICA ONE SILVER DOLLAR PAYABLE TO THE BEARER ON DEMAND.

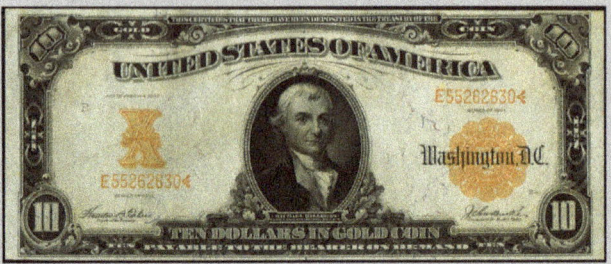

Figure x

Ten-dollar Certificate

"THIS CERTIFIES THAT THERE HAVE BEEN DEPOSITED IN THE TREASURY OF THE UNITED STATES OF AMERICA TEN DOLLARS IN GOLD COIN PAYABLE TO THE BEARER ON DEMAND."

Figure xi

Five-dollar Federal Reserve Note

"FEDERAL RESERVE NOTE THE UNITED STATES OF AMERICA WILL PAY TO THE BEARER ON DEMAND FIVE DOLLARS."

The 1914 Federal Reserve Note in Figure xi is similar in all respects to today's 'fiat' banknotes, in that fiat currency cannot be redeemed against silver or gold coins. Although this information is missing from the note, it is widely understood and accepted.

When fiat money was first introduced, the wording on the notes simply stated that the bearer would be paid the face amount on the note – without stating the basis for such payment. In other words, the issuer of the note does not "back" the notes with something of tangible or internationally-recognised value, such as gold. The claimant would simply be given five one-dollar notes, or coins to the same value. "Backing" means that the bank can only issue a certain value of notes based on the amount of tangible value they have on deposit, usually in the form of gold or silver coins. The certificates of deposit are like that. Fiat money has no such backing – the government simply decrees that the notes have value.

If there is nothing to back the notes, what prevents the issuers from simply printing as many notes as they desire? The answer, of course, is that nothing can stop them, except the government and their regulations. When the issuers do print money in excess, the consequences are dire and are sometimes referred to as 'inflation spiralling out of control'. More information on this subject can be found in Chapter 8.

> ### THE HISTORY OF THE WORD 'DOLLAR'
>
> The word 'dollar' is a corruption of the last two syllables of the German word 'Joachimsthaler' (pronounced *Yo-a-chims-tah-ler*.) 'Joachimsthaler' was the official name of a coin from the silver mine in Joachimsthal (translated as Joachim's Dale or Joachim's Valley) – and was contracted to *thaler*. Joachimsthal is now called 'Jáchymov' and is the name of a town in the modern-day Czech Republic.[8] According to the Oxford English Dictionary, the word '*dollar*' was "… a coin used in the Spanish-American colonies, which was also widely used in the British North American colonies at the time of the American War of Independence, hence adopted as the name of the US monetary unit in the late 18th century."[9]

---

8   The story and pictures of the coin can be found at: http://www.bbc.com/travel/story/20200107-welcome-to-jchymov-the-czech-town-that-invented-the-dollar.

9   Meaning of Dollar in English, Lexico, https://www.lexico.com/definition/dollar

CHAPTER 6

THE VALUE OF TIME

As I was preparing for bed one evening, I recalled my dream of Mercy-the-Merchant's emergency and how she had needed Duckie's help in providing her with forty kilograms of potatoes in a hurry. If you'll remember, Duckie (at the time) owed Mercy ten chickens in exchange for the kilogram of vegetable seeds she had previously asked her for. Mercy had suggested that, since the value of forty kilograms of potatoes was equivalent to four chickens (under normal circumstances), Duckie would then only owe her six (not ten) chickens, after the trade. Duckie had then reminded Mercy that, since it was an emergency, they were not operating under normal circumstances. She had therefore suggested that the only way to make it a fair trade would be for Mercy to reduce the number of chickens Duckie owed her, from a total of six chickens down to five.

Initially, the idea of exchanging "value for value" made perfect sense to me. For a while, I had found the change in value from six chickens to five confusing. I had assumed that the fair value exchange of goods (or services) would always involve the same relative quantities of the goods or services being exchanged. Why was this different?

"Why shouldn't people pay more if they want something special, or if they want it in a rush?" I thought to myself. "If they got themselves into trouble by procrastinating or only remembering to do something at the last minute, then the value of getting out of trouble is higher than the normal value of the trade. Since the demand is instantaneously higher than normal, the price should be higher too."

The more I thought about it, the more it began to make sense to me. Soon enough, sleep came to me, and I began to dream again.

Drennie came to realise that the Edel Lawne philosophy of exchanging value-for-value was more complicated than it was when Buzz Sawyer and Mercy Stockitt had traded packed lunches for roof repairs. It wasn't just *"value-for-value"* – it was *"value-for-value-right-now"*.

Drennie also remembered that, in the early days, foodstuffs could be bartered for quantities of goods, depending on whether or not the food in question was in season. For example, at the time of year when peaches are ripe, *everybody's* peaches are ripe. And *everybody* wants to exchange peaches for other goods. Since the supply of peaches exceeds the demand, the value of the peaches reduces. The value of peaches will only rise again when only a few people have peaches available to sell. Therefore, supply and demand will be the determinant of value from time to time. Drennie felt quite proud of herself for figuring out the concept of "value-right-now".

During the summer, Drennie's arrangement was quite satisfactory – she operated Duckie's LactoBactoBuster to clean the milk urns and bottles, in return for five litres of cream. Scoop turned the cream into ice-cream, and Drennie received two litres of ice-cream to trade for the things she wanted.

"What's going to happen in winter when the people are freezing, and they don't want so much ice-cream?" Drennie wondered.

"Can I make a suggestion, Duckie?" she asked, soon after. "Rather than giving me five litres of cream when I operate your LactoBactoBuster, could you give me Edel-currency or promise-notes instead?"

Duckie raised an eyebrow at the teenager. "Let me think about it," she said.

Duckie didn't want to answer Drennie immediately because (barring a disaster in which all her cows died) she would have the same amount of cream available every week — summer and winter. It suited Duckie to reward Drennie's work with cream. She also knew that winter was approaching and that the demand for ice-cream would soon reduce — which meant that her cream would have a lower value during the cold months.

While it occurred to Duckie that it would perhaps not be possible to sell all the available ice-cream, she knew that the folk of Edel Lawne acknowledged the value of cooperating with one another. Eventually, Duckie and Drennie sat down and began their negotiations.

Duckie opened the conversation. "Drennie," she said, "we originally agreed that your work would be rewarded in the form of cream, and we both know that the cream has a higher value in summer because of the greater demand for ice-cream at that time of year."

Duckie paused. "But we also know that an Edel has the same value all year round."

Drennie nodded. "We both face the same problem," she said. "How have you solved it in the past?"

"I make salted butter and vacuum-pack it in airtight containers," answered Duckie. "It always lasts for a season or two."

Drennie sat and thought for a while, and then she had an idea.

"Well, everybody knows that I am a big strong girl," she said, blushing. "So, let me operate the butter-churn for you. I could use the exercise – and I can do part of the work while I'm supervising your LactoBactoBuster. I'll forego the five litres of cream, and you can pay me the going rate in Edel-currency or promise-notes."

And so, a deal was struck. Nobody would be unduly compromised by seasonal variations in demand for ice-cream, because there was an alternative that allowed the supply to match the demand. And that option could not be available to Drennie unless she cooperated with Duckie.

When I awoke from my dream, I remembered the following principles:

- When purchasing, there is a cost price advantage in buying commodities when supply is high, and demand is low.

- Conversely, when selling, a higher price can be achieved if you can store goods until demand is high and supply is low.

How then could this be turned into a useful enterprise?

That evening, as I dozed off, I felt the stirrings of an embryonic idea.

It made sense to store semi-perishable commodities until demand increased relative to supply, and to then sell them at a higher price. Drennie decided that the only way to make this work would be to obtain a small industrial-scale freezer and combine it with a refrigerated storeroom. She discussed this idea with her mom, and Mercy loved it. Since Mercy was fully aware of Drennie's astute and innovative brain, she asked her daughter to calculate how large this contraption should be.

Drennie scribbled some sums down.

"The chiller section needs to be big enough for all the semi-perishable goods which will sell within about two weeks," she said. "And the freezer section must be large enough to store all the foods that can't be ruined by long-term frozen storage. And mom," she added, "don't think that this is going to be just for Duckie's butter and our ice-cream!"

A month later, and after many revisions, the plans were complete. Buzz Sawyer had also provided an estimate of the direct capital costs, as follows:

- 1000 Edels for the refrigeration equipment
- Another 700 Edels for other costs

Mercy did not have that much money. She could only afford 600 Edels. There was a lucrative and unexploited opportunity sitting right under her nose, but it was unaffordable. She and Drennie were surprised that the 'other costs' could amount to more than two-thirds of the cost of the equipment.

Ever the pragmatic one, Drennie thought about it for a while.

"There is only a need for one freezer-and-cold-room in Edel Lawne," she said to her mom. "If we find a way to build one for our retail business, Duckie might see the benefits and build her own. Then there will be too much capacity, and both businesses may suffer. But, if our retail business and Duckie's can both profit from one freezer-and-cold-room, it's a win-win. Please let me discuss this with Duckie."

Mercy agreed, and a meeting was promptly arranged.

Following the meeting, Drennie reported back:

"Mom, Duckie is excited about the idea, but she can only provide 400 Edels. That gives us enough to buy the refrigeration plant, but it's not enough for all the other costs. I visited the bank, and in principle, they can lend us the other 700 Edels. All they need is a copy of our business plan."

"Well done, Drennie!" said Mercy, beaming with pride. "Let's get moving on the business plan then. We must remember that the bank is only interested in the rate at which we can pay back the loan. That is the calculation they want to see to judge their risk in giving us the loan."

Within a month, Drennie, Mercy and Duckie had prepared a business plan for a new enterprise, to be named EDEL LAWNE COLD STORAGE (PTY) LTD, or ELCS for short. The business plan contained a multitude of details that were required to evaluate the project's economic viability and the bank's risk of providing a loan.

Drennie was astonished at the complexity and the nature of these considerations when contemplating a business venture.

"We live and learn!" she thought to herself. "And now it's easy to see why Buzz Sawyer warned us that 'other costs' could amount to 700 Edels."

The bank was satisfied with the plan and agreed to lend the 700 Edel shortfall to ELCS – but they wanted to use Duckie's LactoBactoBuster as security. This meant that if ELCS failed to repay the loan on time, the bank could apply to the courts to 'seize' the LactoBactoBuster and sell it. That was how the bank would protect themselves against ELCS defaulting on payment. Mercy and Duckie thought about it and decided that the bank's request was reasonable, for two reasons. Firstly, Mercy was risking more of her money in the new venture than Duckie.

Secondly, Duckie would score a quick benefit by cold-storing her excess butter during the winter, which was fast approaching. Mercy, on the other hand, would need more time to build up her stock, so her benefits would only kick in later.

The bank offered them a loan term of three years, an interest rate of 11% per annum, along with a grace period of four months before they had to start making their monthly repayments. The experienced banker also confirmed that ELCS could borrow another 300 Edels to cover any unexpected cost overruns and fund the initial purchases of stock that would be sold down the line. The banker called it "working capital".

"11% interest!" Drennie thought. "Even money has a price."

She baulked at the idea of having to pay interest in addition to repayment of the loan. But then she remembered the maxim *"nothing for nothing"*. Without the bank's 700 Edels – plus the comfort of another 300 Edels to be used if necessary – the project could not go ahead. The loan had value for ELCS, and the bank had to be rewarded for accepting the business risk and for guaranteeing additional capital.

Once the loan was finalised, Mercy and Duckie arranged for a lawyer to draw up the articles of association and a shareholders' agreement, and to register their business. They also hired an accountant to set up the shareholders' register and loan accounts – in other words, a record of how much the company owed to each of the two shareholders, based on the 'seed capital' Mercy and Duckie had provided to start the business. Because of the respective amounts they had each invested, Mercy owned 60% of ELCS, and Duckie owned 40%.

Their accountant also set up the bookkeeping procedures, registered ELCS for payment of income tax and value-added tax, and ensured compliance with all statutory requirements[10].

I awoke as if a bucket of ice water had been emptied over me. My head was spinning with all the concepts Drennie had made use of.

FIRST:

The private sector – in other words, the part of the economy (businesses like ELCS) that is not controlled by government – thrives on identifying wants and needs. That's how they establish a demand for products and services. Demand can be described as an affordable need or want, for example, ice-cream. The private sector is

---

10   This includes legal documentation that governs the operation of the company. Interested readers can investigate the terms "Memorandum and Articles of Association" and "Certificate of Incorporation".

skilled at establishing the best possible prices that the average person can afford for these products and services. Pricing is one of the aspects of professional marketing since people pay what they believe something is worth. Bear in mind that when significantly high prices (and profits) can be achieved, it will attract the immediate interest of competitors. If the cost of production is too high, then it becomes necessary to improve efficiencies (for example, by automating monotonous tasks) to reduce costs.

SECOND:

In the real world of commercial rivalry, competition keeps prices affordable. Profit, even when operating within a competitive environment, is a good thing because it leads to a reserve of available cash. Available cash allows a business to ***choose***[11] from a range of options. If an enterprise has no cash reserves, no ***choices*** are available, and only the cheapest items can be purchased. The business might even be forced to lay off workers or sell off productive equipment or parts of the business. At worst, they might even be forced into bankruptcy with the liquidation of whatever assets remain. Declaring bankruptcy is not really a ***choice***. A forced sale hardly

---

11   In the paragraphs that follow, the word 'choice' (and its variations) are *italicised* and **emboldened** in order to emphasise that profit allows for choice. In the absence of profit, choices are restricted. Strategies and tactics are curtailed. Often, unwelcome outcomes are forced upon businesses that have low profitability.

ever achieves a decent price, even if parts of the assets or profitable parts of the enterprise are put up for sale. Nobody wants to buy a marginal business – in other words, a business that is scraping by and barely making a profit. If a business follows this forced-sale route, the unprofitable and marginal parts of the business remain unsold anyway.

If Duckie's FARM 'n KITCHEN and Mercy's retail enterprise had not been profitable, they would not have been able to ***choose*** to make their contribution of 1000 Edels to start the project, and the bank would not have loaned them the 700 Edels they needed, nor provided the additional 300 Edels facility for working capital.

It's no different on a personal level. I remembered how much Drennie wanted that low-cut dress that Mercy had refused to buy for her. If Drennie had not saved the additional reserve of cash, she would not have been able to ***choose*** to take advantage of the one-day special offer of three dresses for the price of two. Next time you're in a supermarket, examine the price of toilet paper (the same brand and type) when packed individually, and when packaged in packs of three, nine, eighteen, or thirty-six rolls. Normally, the larger the pack-size, the lower the unit price of each toilet roll. Without having excess cash available, you cannot ***choose*** the larger pack with the lower unit price.

THIRD:

Intangible assets, like time, have value too. I realised that Drennie's conclusion about the interest rate being the 'price' of money was only partially correct. The interest cost is a combination of the price (value) of money *and* the price of time. Duckie and Mercy could have **chosen** to wait until their accumulated profits were high enough to fund their cold storage project without a bank loan. But by then, somebody else may have taken advantage of the opportunity. The fact that they had cash available allowed them to **choose** to borrow the shortfall and proceed with the project.

I could never have dreamed (pun intended) how complex a capital project like Mercy's and Duckie's could be.

INTEREST BOX – GOOD DEBT vs BAD DEBT

In the section above, accepting 700 Edels in debt (borrowed to accelerate the refrigeration project) clearly had a beneficial outcome. The debt contributed to the creation of value that was greater than the cost of the debt – in other words, income and profits that would not have been possible without the debt.

This is very different from going into debt to make a 'vanity purchase', such as a flashy car, the newest smartphone, or the latest fashion item— in fact, anything that is just 'nice-to-have'. These depreciating assets decrease in value every month and normally generate no income. Great care must be taken to ensure the affordability of such debt.

At the risk of sounding preachy, before buying a depreciating asset, think carefully about the humorous 1928 definition of *Americanism*: "Using money you haven't earned to buy things you don't need to impress people you don't like."[12]

---

12 Using Money You Haven't Earned To Buy Things You Don't Need To Impress People You Don't Like, Quote Investigator, https://quoteinvestigator.com/2016/04/21/impress/#return-note-13514-1.

CHAPTER 7

RICH MAN, POOR MAN – WHAT IS WEALTH?

"Wake up, you idiots! Whatever made you think paper was so valuable?"

Kurt Vonnegut, Galápagos

Readers will recall that I had not scored well in Economics at school. I was determined to show a positive response to my teacher's comments that usually read *"Can do better"* and *"Must try harder"*.

My economics assignment read as follows:

"In 250 to 300 words, discuss hoarding (also called 'panic buying'), price gouging and rationing as responses to food shortages following a disaster."

I had already begun my research when I remembered my dream about Drennie inventing the golden Edel as a store of value. At the time, I saw the Edels as wealth, but now I had some doubts. Rare commodities like precious metals and cowrie shells are merely tokens that are useful for exchanging value or storing it for a while – they are not *embodiments* of wealth. The person who owns the tokens may believe that the tokens have value, but until the person receiving the tokens sees the value in them, the tokens have no value at all.

So, what is wealth?

I was convinced that wealth is not money – money is nothing more than a token of wealth, and its value is relative. The value of money changes based on time, place and context.

As sleep came to me, a nightmare began.

The tempest broke over the tranquil village of Edel Lawne at four o'clock one afternoon. It began as a powerful thunderstorm, but, after an hour, it became clear that something was terribly wrong. Gigantic drops of rain interspersed with hail continued to fall, drumming interminably on the roofs of Edel Lawne's buildings. As night fell, lightning streaked through the darkness.

Thunder cracked and crashed as the rain grew more and more violent, and the wind screamed an unholy chorus.

A rumbling came from the direction of the river where the villagers panned for gold dust and nuggets. Boulders, each one the size of a small car, were being driven downstream by the force of the water, grinding and crushing everything in their path. The villagers opened the dam's sluice gates, but this did little to manage the water's flow. By ten o'clock that night, the dam had overflowed and completely collapsed. The power plant was swamped, and the lights went out. Water began flooding through the streets of Edel Lawne, pushing its way under the doors of houses and businesses.

The storm did not abate until after midnight and, as morning broke, the townsfolk began to understand the enormity of what had befallen their beloved village. Many of the houses and commercial buildings had been damaged. Buzz Sawyer would be busy with repairs for months. A large portion of Duckie Planter's agricultural fields had been washed away and the crops had suffered devastating damage. Even more distressing was the fact that many of her livestock had drowned – only two roosters and four hens had survived the flood. Nothing remained of the town's water purification plant which had been in the path of the boulders forced downstream by the floodwaters. A shortage of food and safe drinking water immediately became apparent.

Drennie assessed the situation and quickly identified the risks of two important and connected phenomena – *hoarding* and *price gouging*.

- **HOARDING**

    Everyone who arrived first at Mercy's retail supply points and Duckie's FARM 'N KITCHEN – especially the rich – would buy up all of the available supplies, since nobody knew when replacement stocks would become available.

    Buying far more than one needs is known as "hoarding". It results in the logical but non-uniform distribution of limited resources. In other words, while it made sense for people to panic, all the supplies would be sitting in the hands of those few people who had managed to get their hands on what was left to buy.

- **PRICE GOUGING**

    The normal laws of supply and demand indicate that as demand increases (through hoarding), businesses selling these products will increase their prices to take advantage of the sudden demand. Under disaster conditions, an extreme increase in price like this is known as price gouging. Such profiteering is illegal in some countries.

Logically, under these circumstances, Mercy and Duckie *should* increase the prices of their goods – not because they want to profit off the townsfolk's misfortunes, but because they themselves would experience delays in replenishing these goods. The delays would be caused by a damaged supply chain – for example, Duckie lost all her cattle in the floods, so milk (and ice-cream) would be in short supply until she was able to buy more cows. If she managed to source milk and cream from a farmer in a nearby village, she would have to pay more for that milk than it would cost her to produce, and her prices would naturally have to increase. If Mercy and Duckie did not raise their prices, they would not have enough money to buy sufficient amounts of the more expensive replacement stock they needed.

Their higher prices could also act as a deterrent to townsfolk buying up excessive quantities of anything they could lay their hands on and hoarding it for later.

As these shocking scenarios passed through Drennie's mind, she asked herself how these two situations could be avoided. What would constitute an equitable course of action? Edel Lawne was a small enough community that everyone knew everyone else. Because of their nothing-for-nothing philosophy and their belief in exchanging value for value, the townsfolk trusted one another, they had high ethical standards, and there was a culture of cooperation amongst them. The ensuing weeks would remind the villagers of how valuable these philosophies were, since they would allow them to adopt a course of action that few other communities could have done.

Immediately after checking that everybody in Edel Lawne was safe, the villagers called a meeting to discuss a recovery plan. Drennie was loved and respected by the townsfolk. She had, after all, explained the puzzle of the shrinking Edels and the promise-note that Georgie had forged, but on which he had spelt "Stockitt" wrongly. It was only natural that when Drennie said she had some ideas, the villagers were willing to listen. This is what she suggested:

- A committee must assess everyone's immediate needs and administer the recovery plan.
- The committee would have two days to assess and respond to the destruction, prioritising the most serious and urgent of the damages suffered in their scheduling of repairs.
- Essential requirements must be strictly rationed.
- During those first two days – and longer if necessary – the usual philosophy of nothing-for-nothing would still apply, but rewards would be based on "Emergency Recordal Notes", to be issued by the committee. These notes would be like the old-fashioned signed promise-notes indicating supplier and consumer, and serving as records of goods and services that were needed and supplied during the emergency. Only the

quantity of goods or services was to be shown on the notes – no values or prices.

- By implication, the practice of paying for goods and services with promise-notes or Edels was to be suspended with immediate effect.
- Reward for goods and services provided would be delayed until normality had returned.
- Reward would be based on the prices at which replacement goods were purchased (for the purpose of resale by suppliers) *after* the emergency.
- At the end of the two days, the villagers were to meet again and decide on further courses of action.

In one way, the Emergency Recordal Notes would be like the ration cards used during times of war. In another way, they were a bit like food stamp programmes that allow low-income and no-income families to buy basic foodstuffs.

The first person to seek the right to procure goods and services was Duckie Planter. In the cooperative spirit that pervaded Edel Lawne, doing so would not be for her benefit alone. In the spirit of teamwork, her argument to the committee was as follows:

"The power plant is down and will be for days. The food in our freezer will soon be rotten. Most of my chickens are dead, but they are still fresh. If I don't cook the food and the dead hens right away, they will all go to waste. My problem is that I don't have enough fuel for my stoves.

I require the right to receive enough fuel to cook all the dead chickens and all the food in the ELCS freezer and cold storage. Also, I need fuel to cook whatever can be saved from my damaged crops. Then, at least there will be some food available in Edel Lawne. Lastly, I will need additional fuel to boil the river water, to make it safe for drinking until the water-treatment plant is repaired."

The committee granted this right and wrote out the first "Emergency Recordal Note". Soon the townsfolk were referring to such a note as an "ERN". They pronounced it to rhyme with "earn", emphasising their philosophy of nothing-for-nothing.

Duckie took the ERN to Mercy's store, received the fuel, and soon she was cooking up a storm using the damaged crops and dead chickens, and the food from ELCS. She used another ERN to procure vegetable seeds and planted them immediately.

The storm had not damaged the neighbouring town as badly, so it was possible to procure goods from there. Money-promise-notes were not recognised in that town, but gold coins were. The committee authorised the issuing of golden Edels to Mercy, and she led a delegation of townsfolk to procure emergency goods in the town down the road.

Within a few weeks, the surviving but traumatised hens began laying eggs again, and the vegetables were sprouting. After the emergency, Mercy took the ERNs to the committee and was compensated in Edels to the extent of the replacement value of the fuel and seeds. The long path to recovery had begun, and the value of their philosophy of cooperation amongst the townsfolk was reinforced.

The emergency also taught the people of Edel Lawne that wealth does not equal money.

I awoke in a cold sweat, deeply saddened by the misfortune that had befallen the dream-characters that I had come to regard as my friends. As distraught as I was, I was particularly proud of Drennie, knowing that her thought processes were indeed my own. Plus, I had the framework for my economics assignment.

I realised that 'the rich' can survive disasters more comfortably than 'the poor'. People with money can pay the exorbitant prices that unscrupulous price gougers might charge for scarce commodities. The rich can afford to hoard non-perishable goods. But would their wealth benefit them if there was simply no product available to buy? In a simplistic view, one may believe that wealth is characterised by access to money (or credit), but under extreme conditions, a different definition is required. When the storerooms are empty, and the market shelves are bare, and there is no food whatsoever, knowing how to hunt and cook rats is worth more than a kilogram of gold. The person who can do that has a saleable skill – and saleable rats – no matter whether they're raw or cooked.

I came up with the following clumsy definition that captures the gist of the lesson learned by the villagers:

"Wealth is that which most closely guarantees current and future physical and emotional wellbeing."

> **HISTORICAL INTEREST BOX – COVID-19**
>
> Most of this work was written before the coronavirus pandemic broke out in 2020. Readers will undoubtedly empathise with the hoarding and price gouging that took place – especially when it came to profiteering from the sale of toilet paper, hand sanitiser and face masks. The South African National Consumer Commission (NCC) prosecuted multiple companies for price gouging.
>
> Interestingly, when evaluating profit margins to consider the acceptability of the huge jump in prices, the NCC apparently only takes *historical* costs and prices into account and not future replacement costs.

Reader, you have three tasks:

1) Dream up (pun intended) your own definition of wealth that applies under all circumstances.

2) Read the last paragraph in the COVID-19 Historical Interest Box. Does the Commission's policy make sense morally and economically? Explain the reasons for your answer.

3) Pretend you are the teacher, and you have to grade my work. Here is the topic of my assignment again: *"In 250 to 300 words, discuss hoarding (also called panic buying), price gouging, and rationing as responses to food shortages following a disaster."*

This is what I wrote:

There is an argument that price gouging does not exist – that it is simply a reaction to supply and demand. Goods are offered for sale at a price. If the price is too high, people will not buy.

(Reference: <http://economics.fundamentalfinance.com/price-gouging.php>).

But that is too simplistic an answer. The two phenomena – hoarding and price gouging – are interactive: If price rises are restricted by laws intended to prevent price gouging, hoarding is encouraged. In response to the risk that there may be nothing of a given commodity available in the future, people will buy everything they can afford. The rich will buy more than the poor, which they usually do anyway. Per capita *consumption by the rich is (logically) higher than that of the poor. Driven by the fear of expected scarcity, the rich are inclined to buy far more than they need, and the retail shelves will quickly empty.*

Had the prices simply been allowed to rise organically in response to scarcity (or increased demand), the shelves would have stayed stocked for longer because price rises diminish consumption. When retail shelves are empty, starvation stares into the faces of all – the rich and the poor. Hungry people are tempted to resort to extreme measures and may engage in looting as the shelves approach emptiness – simply because those with disposable cash bought far more than they needed.

If prices are allowed to rise in response to scarcity, the rich will be able to buy, while the poor cannot. The risk of violence in response to hunger is the same, but price rises will deter even the rich from hoarding more than they need – and the authorities will have more time to react.

Physical rationing seems to be the only way to resolve the dilemma equitably.

Reader, what grade did you give me for my assignment? Please justify your grading.

CHAPTER 8

...BEGGARMAN, THIEF

I was becoming quite used to having dreams about trade, wealth and matters relating to money, but my next dream was vastly more complicated than the others.

Drennie recalled how Georgie Ford had shaved the edges off the golden Edels and forged one of Mercy's promise-notes. She also remembered how the kindly – or perhaps gullible – villagers of Edel Lawn had forgiven him and allowed him to stay. Georgie was aloof towards her – almost rude, probably because he knew that she was still suspicious of him. It was as if he knew that she had nicknamed him *Georgie Fraud*. That didn't worry Drennie one little bit; she knew that she was in charge of *that* relationship. Having minimal contact with Georgie suited her just fine. In fact, if she never met him again, that would also be too soon.

Georgie was soon joined by twenty-year-old Claude Treacher. Shortly after Claude arrived in Edel Lawne, Drennie spotted him and Georgie passing by the door of the ice-cream works. Despite her misgivings about Georgie – and since Drennie was always well-mannered – she greeted them as they walked past. Georgie acknowledged her with a curt nod, but Claude smiled at her, looked straight into her eyes, and asked, "What's your name?"

"Dren…" the first syllable came out as a high-pitched squeak as Drennie's larynx constricted. Why the heck was her fifteen-year-old heart hammering away like that, she wondered? She felt utterly dizzy. The truth is, she had never seen anyone as handsome as Claude in her entire life. She cleared her throat, recovered her composure a little and said in her most grown-up tone, "I'm Drennie Stockitt. Have you come for an ice-cream?"

"We're busy," said Georgie Ford bluntly, brushing her off.

"Well, I will certainly come by for one later," Claude smiled, setting Drennie's heart aflutter all over again.

After a few weeks, Claude opened a business. He was a skilled manufacturing jeweller, and the people of Edel Lawne liked his work. Since they were proud of their gold

Edels, they handed them to Claude to have them set in pendant necklaces, rings and earrings. Claude stored the Edels that people brought to him in a heavy steel safety vault until he was ready to set them. In addition to the safe's regular lock, it also had a time-lock that prevented the door from being opened for half an hour after the combination lock was released. If any robbers were to pay him a visit, the time-lock would give the law-enforcement authorities (like Strike Klopper) a chance to arrive before the robbers got their dirty hands on the Edels.

In the beginning, Claude's customers would ask him for a receipt stating what he had received from them, but Claude was a smooth talker. He persuaded them to accept a redeem-note, which stated that he had the Edels on deposit in his vault and that they could be recovered on presentation of the redeem-note. When Claude gave them their jewellery, they would return the redeem-notes – all of which bore his signature – to him. Soon, the townsfolk began depositing their golden Edels in Claude's vault for safe-keeping. In their minds, the redeem-note was as good as gold.

The redeem-notes were all similar to one another; two of them looked like this:

> **I, Claude Treacher, have on deposit and redeemable against this note: TWO EDELS**
> *Claude Treacher*

> **I, Claude Treacher, have on deposit and redeemable against this note: TEN EDELS**
> *Claude Treacher*

Since an Edel was equal to one month's wages, Claude's redeem-notes were regularly tendered as payment for large transactions. Drennie (with her fluttering heart) didn't mind that Claude seemed to have copied her promise-notes. If anything, she took it as a compliment.

"We're a good match," she thought dreamily.

She collected her promise-notes studiously while minding Mercy's store and operating Duckie's LactoBactoBuster. She also saved the coins from her ice-cream sales until she had enough to exchange for a golden Edel. That golden Edel gave her the perfect opportunity to saunter into Claude's jewellery-works and ask him, in the most grown-up manner possible, to accept her deposit in exchange for a redeem-note. And of course, she would only go there when she was certain that Claude was in attendance.

Mercy's and Drennie's stores-of-value increasingly took on the form of Claude's redeem-notes. Drennie slept with hers under her pillow to have Claude's signature close to her cheek, oblivious to the skulduggery brewing in the background. The people of Edel Lawne seemed to have forgotten that Claude's partner was Georgie Ford, the promise-note forger and coin-shaver. Georgie, in the meantime, was keeping to himself in the shadows of Claude's jewellery works.

"George," said Claude one day, "I think we can make some extra money if we charge a small fee for safe-keeping Edels. Since it's a service of value and the townsfolk of Edel Lawne all agree about exchanging value for value, I don't think they'll have a problem paying us for this valuable service."

What Claude didn't know was that Georgie had also been thinking about the safekeeping of Edels. His scheme, however, was much grander – and thoroughly dishonest.

"How many people know exactly how many Edels are stored in our vault?" Georgie asked.

"Two," said Claude. "You and me."

"And how many people know how many redeem-notes you have given out?"

"Two," said Claude. "You and me."

"Apart from the redeem-notes that come back to us when people collect their jewellery, how many people come to give back their notes and reclaim their Edels from us?"

Claude scratched his chin. Claude had (admittedly) noticed that unless they were collecting jewellery, hardly anybody in the village was presenting their redeem-notes in exchange for their Edels. They were simply being used in the same way as promise-notes, as a form of payment. After all, weren't the redeem notes as good as gold?

"Almost none, Georgie – why do you ask?"

"I ask, my dear unimaginative friend, because your highly imaginative partner, I - Georgie Ford - have discovered the world's best-kept secret."

"And what secret is that, Georgie?"

"I have discovered that *nothing-for-nothing* is nothing but a whole lot of nonsense! Baloney! Hogwash!" blurted Georgie. "Write a redeem-note for one Edel. We're going out for dinner. We'll pay with the redeem-note and accept change in coinage or Edel-promise-notes. Now *that's* value. And we'll get it for nothing!"

Claude thought about the idea, and a grin spread across his face. For all his good looks, he was a gullible young man.

The adage *"If it seems too good to be true, it probably is"* was not only true for Georgie and Claude but for all the people of Edel Lawne. Bit by bit, the townsfolk started noticing that the number of redeem-notes required in exchange for a fixed quantity of goods or services was rising. Were the redeem notes really as good as gold? The value of their beloved and respected golden Edels was in jeopardy, but nobody could understand what was causing their mysterious reduction in value. All the while, Claude and Georgie seemed to have money to burn, flaunting more money than would be realistic to have earned for the amount of jewellery business which they were doing.

Some weeks later, several of Edel Lawne's traders needed to procure goods in the neighbouring town. While the golden Edels were accepted as tokens of value there, Claude's redeem-notes were not. Drennie was to accompany Scoop Cooper to the neighbouring town to buy a new ice-cream machine. He, Mercy and the other traders all queued up at the jewellery works and presented their redeem-notes to Claude. Drennie had brought along her stash of beloved notes from under her pillow, bearing the signature of "gorgeous Claude", as she secretly called him. Reluctantly, she was going to be forced to convert them back into golden Edels.

"WHADDAYAMEAN – *'NOT ENOUGH EDELS'?*"

The accusatory question blared out from just inside the door of the jewellery shop. A flustered, red-faced Claude had just broken the unfortunate news that there were not enough Edels to honour all the redeem-notes.

"I don't know where Georgie is," he stammered. "He must have left town and taken the Edels with him!"

When the queue started to form at the jewellery shop that morning, Georgie Ford had quickly realised that their fraudulent scheme was about to be exposed. Strike Klopper had chased him out of town with a red-hot iron rod once before, and he wasn't about to risk being brandished with it again. Georgie had shaved pieces off the Edels, he'd forged a promise-note, and now he'd created fraudulent redeem-notes backed by nothing at all. He was a good enough judge of character to realise that even the villagers of Edel Lawne would not forgive him a third time. He had slipped away as the queue began to form and was never seen again.

Claude, in the meantime, was doing everything he could to avoid admitting that he and Georgie had issued far more redeem-notes than the number of golden Edels they were safe-keeping. Drennie had been suspicious of Georgie Ford ever since she had caught him shaving pieces off the golden Edels and forging Mercy's milk promise-note. She had a strong feeling that he had been up to no good again. And since Claude was his friend, she now had no doubt that the two of them had conspired to defraud the townsfolk.

"Just a minute!" she called out, making her way towards the front of the queue. "We're going to get to the bottom of this right here and now. We're going to start by calculating the value of everybody's redeem-notes, and then we're going to count how many Edels are in the vault. Those numbers should be the same."

"Good idea!" the assembled villagers chorused, moving towards the table Drennie had fetched from inside the jewellery shop. The townsfolk recognised a good leader when they saw one, even if she was only fifteen years old.

"Strike," Drennie shouted, "please keep an eye on Claude before he walks out the back door."

Her once-fluttering heart was now pounding over the enormity of what Claude had done. Her heart was in pieces, and she felt utterly betrayed.

Strike put his boot down firmly on Claude's left foot. "Don't even think about sneaking out, Claude *Treacherous*," he muttered, grinding his heel in a little harder than he should have.

As soon as the time-lock released the vault's door, Drennie and Claude – watched closely by Strike and a few other worthies – counted the Edels one by one and compared them with the redeem-notes. The result of the counting-up was thus:

Edels recorded on all the redeem-notes:	7000
Edels in the vault:	3500

"There's nothing we can do," said Drennie, addressing the crowd. "I suggest we all take half the number of Edels shown on our redeem-notes."

"But that's not fair!" complained one of the villagers who had just deposited ten golden Edels the day before. "I only get half of what Claude owes me."

"Do you have a better suggestion?" Drennie asked. "The damage can't be reversed. We don't know which redeem-notes refer to which Edels. I had a feeling that some of the Edels might have been stolen. But the time-lock still had not released the vault's door, so I don't think Georgie or Claude had time to steal the Edels today. They didn't know until this morning that we would all want to withdraw our golden Edels at the same time."[13]

The villagers all agreed that there had never been 7000 Edels in the vault, and were left with no choice but to agree with Drennie's suggestion. The notes were all deemed to

---

13   This is a phenomenon similar to a "run on the bank". See https://www.investopedia.com/terms/b/bankrun.asp for a description of this form of "bank panic" and its consequences.

be backed by the Edels on deposit to the extent of 50%. They had all learned a very expensive lesson.

The villagers marched to Claude's house and collected his bed, carrying it down the road to Strike's workshop. Once it was inside, they chained Claude to it and locked him in. Drennie cried herself to sleep that night.

The following morning, Drennie watched as the villagers expelled Claude from Edel Lawne.

"*...and NEVER COME BACK!*" they shouted as he trudged away, stoop-shouldered with nothing but the clothes on his back.

Drennie was filled with mixed emotions. While she was angry at what Georgie had done and how he had abused Claude's naivety, she was disappointed that Claude had been so easily led astray. Most of all, she was irritated that the villagers had allowed Georgie to remain in Edel Lawne after he had scammed them the second time with the forged promise-note. She wanted to yell, "I knew we shouldn't have let him back!"

"Well," she acknowledged silently to herself, "nobody promised me that life would be fair. I'll simply add this episode to my store of experience. We live, and we learn."

Not long afterwards, the townsfolk turned the jewellery works into the village's first bank.

> **INFORMATION BOX – INFLATION:**
>
> What happened in Edel Lawne is known as inflation. With too much (devalued) money (quantity of redeem-notes) chasing too little value, the prices of goods and services rose.
>
> *Caveat*: While it was viable to measure the effect of inflation in the imaginary town by reconciling the golden Edels against Claude's redeem-notes, it is not possible to do this in the real world. Since every country's central bank[14] controls the money supply (directed by the government), the only way to control the amount of fiat currency being created is to control the country's central bank.
>
> By doing as Georgie Ford suggested, Claude initiated a procedure that has been widely practised throughout the world ever since banks came into existence. Even before fiat money made an appearance in the twentieth century, currency-issuing banks have printed more paper money than they had funds on deposit, or tokens — usually gold or silver — in their vaults.
>
> Why, you may ask, does this practice continue? Do its negative effects not lead to inflation?

---

14   Most countries have their own central bank. Three examples are the Bank of England (UK), the South African Reserve Bank and the Federal Reserve (USA). Today, they issue only fiat money – backing with other tokens of value (such as gold or silver) is not required.

High inflation, as we saw happen in this chapter, is a bad outcome. Conventional wisdom is that zero inflation also has a bad outcome, since zero inflation inhibits economic growth because there is no incentive to buy today what you can buy for the same price next year. Delayed spending leads to a contraction of the economy. Thus, having some inflation is desirable, especially if it is only a few percent. In South Africa, for example, the inflation target is between 3% and 6% per annum.

So, inflation is a natural consequence of a healthy economy. For simplicity, we'll use GDP ("Gross Domestic Product" — the value of all the goods and services produced by a country) as the determinant to be measured. When inflation is kept under control at a low percentage, the real economic growth (the creation of new real value) outweighs the negative effects of inflation. This means that the economy (the total wealth of the country) is growing faster than the inflation rate. For example, if the nominal growth rate (without taking inflation into account) is 10% and the inflation rate is 4%, there is 6% greater real wealth in the economy in the current year than in the previous year. Various terms are used for this inflation-adjusted value, including "constant-price,", "inflation-corrected", or "constant dollar" GDP.[15]

---

15   Akhilesh Ganti, Real Gross Domestic Product (GDP), Investopedia,
https://www.investopedia.com/terms/r/realgdp.asp#:~:text=Key%20Takeaways,or%20%22constant%20dollar%22%20GDP

The government – or more correctly, the dominant political party that controls the government – wants the economy to grow so that more and more value is created, along with more and more jobs, thereby giving the people a better quality of life. When a government achieves this, they are more likely to be voted back into power at the next election. More money loaned out means more expenditure, which means more economic activity. Eventually, the increased economic activity manifests itself as more wealth for the people. Higher personal income translates into higher tax revenue that the government can use to fulfil promises made during their election campaigns.

Interested readers are encouraged to investigate the tools a central bank can use to control the money supply.

Consider starting at https://www.stlouisfed.org/in-plain-english/how-monetary-policy-works.

However, when the money supply is not properly restrained, inflation can spiral out of control. In countries where a high standard of governance exists, the central bank is intentionally kept at arm's length from party-political influence. In countries where the opposite exists, you will generally find the unrestrained printing of banknotes without the backing of additional underlying value (commensurate with production in the economy), leading to hyperinflation.

Just imagine how the following two scenarios would have

influenced the investment decision process for Mercy and Duckie in Chapter 6. Note especially the interest rate of 35% mentioned below compared to the 11% per annum interest they were charged. Investment decisions are wickedly risky in such an inflation environment.

Hyperinflation is where too many notes are chasing a constrained quantity of goods. Two examples of this are what happened in Germany in the 1920s, and in Zimbabwe in the years leading up to 2008/2009 – and again in 2020.

Nearly a hundred years ago, inflation in Germany was exacerbated when workers in the Ruhr valley in the Weimar Republic went on a general strike in 1923, and the German government printed more money to continue paying for their passive resistance. Towns and cities printed their own vouchers for value backed by nothing. By November of that year, the United States dollar was worth 4,210,500,000,000 German marks, with notes of higher and higher values being required. It got so bad that one needed a wheelbarrow full of notes to buy one loaf of bread.

Figure xii

Translation: Voucher worth fifty trillion marks "Billionen" in German means a million-million, which we know in English as a trillion.

The vouchers were issued by the cities Eschweiler and Stolberg.

In 2009, Zimbabwe abandoned its currency, the Zimbabwean dollar, which had become virtually worthless because of the uncontrolled printing of currency. The ubiquitous means of exchange were the United States Dollar and the more stable currencies of surrounding countries, including the South African rand, the Botswana pula and the Namibian dollar. The banknote in Figure xiii shows the consequence, shortly before the government abandoned its currency in favour of the currencies referred to above.

Figure xiii

One hundred trillion Zimbabwean dollar note

See the phrase *"I promise to pay the bearer on demand"*, derived from the promise-note concept described in Chapter 5.

The Zimbabwean dollar was re-introduced in 2019, and inflation made its presence felt again. In November 2020, the annual inflation rate in the country was more than 400%. An item that cost one dollar in January cost more than four dollars by December of the same year. To compensate for this, the Reserve Bank of Zimbabwe applied an interest rate of 35% per annum on their loans to commercial banks.[16] The commercial banks then offered loans to their customers at an even higher interest rate, crippling the economy since businesses had to make

---

16   Trading Economics, Zimbabwe Interest Rate Summary, https://tradingeconomics.com/zimbabwe/interest-rate .

even higher profits to be able to repay their loans.

Here is a final thought on the subject of fiat money, inflation and economic wellbeing: The capitalist 'story' is about growth – the creation of ever-increasing quantities of goods and services to balance the increased creation of fiat money. According to Yuval Noah Harari, *"The answer to all problems, the key to all the questions that bother us, is economic growth. No matter what you want in the long term, the only way to achieve it is [through] economic growth. You want equality, you want freedom, you want employment, you want democracy, you want peace – [you] name it, it's through economic growth. And if there will not be economic growth, in the long run, you won't have any of that."*[17]

---

17   Yuval Noah Harari, *The Myths We Need to Survive*, Intelligence Squared, thirty-two minutes into the video at https://www.youtube.com/watch?v=UTchioiHM0U.

CHAPTER 9

SMART MONEY

That night, my school materialised in the town of Edel Lawne, with Drennie as one of its pupils.

It was lunch break on Drennie's first day back at school after the holidays. Drennie had been struggling to fit into her low-cut dresses and decided that she was going to put herself on a healthy eating plan. Mercy promised not to leave any ice-cream out to tempt Drennie when she arrived home from school. The only problem was that the school tuckshop made the most delicious cheeseburgers and it had been weeks since she had last sunk her teeth into one of them…

"Cheeseburger, here I come," Drennie thought. "I'll start my diet tomorrow." She picked up her phone, accessed her money-app, gazed delightedly at the balance, and made her way to the front of the tuckshop queue. Mercy had loaned Drennie the money because she had been unable to operate the LactoBactoBuster over at Duckie's place while she was out of town for the holidays. No work – no pay. Nothing for nothing. Drennie had promised to repay the loan at the end of that month.

"A double cheeseburger with fries and a large Coke, please, ma'am."

"That'll be 30 tenks," said the tuckshop attendant as she finalised ringing up the order on the cash register. "I've sent the cost notification to your phone."

"Okay, I see it," said Drennie, glancing down at her phone. "I'm transferring the payment now, ma'am."

There was a pause as Drennie tapped at the screen. Her irritation turned to worry as she repeatedly tapped the 'PAY NOW' icon.

"It won't go through," she said in dismay.

"Hmm, I see the trouble," said the attendant. "My system is rejecting your transaction because you're trying to pay with programmed Edels. "

"Programmed for what? " Drennie asked, wide-eyed.

"The system says *These funds good for health-foods only.* " said the attendant.

Drennie looked down at her phone and the same message appeared. She glared at the screen as if it had done her a sneaky, personal injustice.

"What's on the health-food menu today, ma'am?" Drennie asked quietly, blushing and contrite.

Drennie carried her meal to a table next to the sports field. It was a lunch of Greek salad with a low-calorie dressing, laced with strips of grilled chicken breast. She had chosen fresh orange juice to drink. She smiled in silent admiration for her mother.

"Mom," she thought, "you know me so well. I didn't even know that the tuckshop had categorised the foods in this way. Programmable Edels sure add a brand new meaning to the phrase *smart money*."

INFORMATION BOX – BLOCKCHAIN, CRYPTOCURRENCIES and SMART CONTRACTS

"Everything should be made as simple as possible, but no simpler."

Albert Einstein

It is not easy to provide a simple description of blockchain and cryptocurrencies. The know-how and its applications are changing and growing all the time at a rapid rate. It's rather like a jigsaw puzzle being completed from the inside out, without a picture of the completed image as a guide. Except, with a jigsaw puzzle, at least you know how many pieces are left. With blockchain and cryptocurrencies, we have no idea where these technologies are ultimately going to take us. [18]

So, how close to reality was the episode of programmed Edels in this chapter? Using 'smart contracts' and cryptocurrency, it is technically feasible. It would be a simple matter of coding the values in the child's wallet to provide a small amount each day for sugary, fatty or salty treats, and a larger amount for healthy foods. In

---

18   An extensive addendum to this section is available as a free download from the ResearchGate website. The title is "BLOCKCHAIN, CRYPTOCURRENCIES and CONJECTURE about CROSS-FERTILIZATION with OTHER NOVEL TECHNOLOGIES". Visit http://dx.doi.org/10.13140/RG.2.2.35990.47685

the environment of a school tuckshop, achieving buy-in from the school would be easy since most parents would be happy that their children would be restricted from buying too much junk food.

Smart contracts are not simple either, and the term is misleading, but this is a good description:

"A 'smart contract' is a computer code, which unlike most, isn't installed on a personal computer or a server," explains Pablo F. Burgueño, Chief Legal Officer at Nevtrace, a company that has advised the European Commission on smart contracts and cryptocurrencies. *"The code is registered in a blockchain so it cannot be erased or edited."*[19]

A smart contract will state, for instance, that if and when "A" occurs, "B" must be executed. For example, a smart contract for a life assurance policy could state the following: *"When John dies, release ten thousand dollars to his estate."*

Reliable sources of information about "A" are called oracles. In the case of John's life assurance policy, "A" could be the statutory registry of births and deaths in John's country of citizenship. Since the contract is coded into the blockchain such that it cannot be changed, it is executed without human intervention. As soon as John's

---

19   BBVA, What are Smart Contracts? Five Key Questions, Banco Bilbao Vizcaya Argentaria, S.A, https://www.bbva.com/en/smart-contracts-five-key-questions/

death is registered (this being "A"), the release of monies (being "B") is automatically triggered.

CHAPTER 10

FUTURE-PROOFING

"I would rather have questions that can't be answered than answers that can't be questioned."

Richard Feynman, American physicist

At last! My economics teacher decided to teach us something modern for a change. Today's lesson was about the risks and consequences of the demand for better and quicker technologies. It was quite a long lesson, with more storytelling than teaching, and it went something like this:

It is usually the shortest time to market that determines the success of any new product. The longer it takes to get your product out there, the more chance you have of somebody else coming up with the same idea or copying yours, or for your market to disappear completely. However, taking the time to think is more important now than it ever was. It's important to identify the maximum number of 'what if's' and to design protection against mishaps into the new concepts at an early stage. Fixing them later may be technically impossible or expensive. The consequences of a wrong decision can be instantaneous in today's technological era, leaving less time to take corrective action before irreparable damage is done to your brand's image or through excessive wasted expenditure.

In our modern world, it isn't always possible to take the time to consider everything that could possibly go wrong with a new product or service while still being first to bring it to market.

As an example of the speed and consequential severity of mistakes today (compared to a decade ago), consider the smart contracts described in the information box at the end of Chapter 9. It is almost impossible to fix a mistake in the code because of the 'immutability' (unchangeability) of blockchain technology – you've *"gotta get it right the first time"*. Once blockchain code has been written, you can't go back and change it later. Experts claim that 'escape windows' (conditions pre-programmed into the smart contract's codebase[20]) can allow changes to be made, but this defeats the elegant simplicity of immutable blockchain

---

20   See glossary.

code. This is an example of the increased severity of a mistake compared to simpler times past.

Also, the consequences are more dreadful than in the past — the scale of modern things is greater than was the case historically. The DAO project is an example. Crowdfunding was used to launch the Decentralized Autonomous Organization (DAO). By May 2016, they had raised a staggering US$150-million – the world record for a crowdfunding campaign at that time. A hacker (or hackers) discovered an error or errors in the DAO's codebase and exploited the mistake. Within the first few hours of the attack, the hackers stole the cryptocurrency equivalent of tens of millions of US dollars. That was 'smart theft' on a grand scale.

Interestingly, the scoundrels may not have benefitted to the full value of the theft. Unless the hackers converted the cryptocurrency to fiat money within hours of attacking the DAO, they would have been taking a great risk by attempting to trade any of the ill-gotten gains at a later stage. The DAO's codebase for the smart contracts was built on the Ethereum cryptocurrency (a competitor to Bitcoin) and, since the Ethereum blockchain is not corrupted, the thieves' transaction (if conducted later) would have immediately been flagged as fraudulent. If the hackers tried to convert the cryptos to fiat money immediately after stealing them, it is possible that the commercial bank's fraud department would have identified the transactions as suspicious.[21]

The bell rang to end the lesson before we could ask any questions, and my head was buzzing with them. While I understood that a shorter time to market leads to an increased risk of errors, we were yet to learn how to address the problem. *How do we plan for the dangers*, I asked myself? I wondered if Drennie would come to my rescue with an answer.

All my dreams so far had been visualisations of well-documented historical occurrences based on the chronological development of commerce, industry and economics. But my dream about electronic Edels that were programmed only for purchasing healthy food brought me a half-step into the future. Suddenly, there was a sense of vagueness in Drennie's world, leaving her somewhat uncertain about what might come next. I thought about my future too. How would I earn a living one day?

I couldn't help but wonder where all these new technologies were headed. I wouldn't be surprised if my next dream were to transcend the present and explore the wondrous challenges of the future.

---

21   Internet security is beyond the scope of this book but I'll advise as follows: Learn and keep on learning and apply your knowledge – it's the best form of protection. If you are unfamiliar with this type of risk, search the internet for the phrase "Solarwinds fiasco".

Sure enough, as soon as I dropped off to sleep, my school materialised in Edel Lawne. Drennie was attending a class called "Future-Proofing". It was so different. At my school in the real world, the teachers weren't teaching us how to think – they were simply teaching us how to pass our exams. Nobody at a job interview ever asks you to demonstrate that you are familiar with the square on the hypotenuse, or to recite a Shakespearean sonnet. The interviewer's questions are way more complicated than that. The interviewer might frown upon you if you have not prepared to answer a question about dealing with an uncooperative co-worker – they simply don't teach you this real-world stuff in school.

The only thing Drennie didn't like about the future-proofing class was that the class was so short – only two hours, once a week was far too little time, as far as she was concerned. She loved that there were no right or wrong answers and that she had to defend her conclusions with logic. There was never any psychobabble – simply a reference to a set of facts or opinions for the students to explore, evaluate, criticise and build upon. It allowed them to learn about themselves, about each other, and about life – and the world – beyond everything that was familiar to them.

Another reason that Drennie loved the future-proofing course was because of how the classes were made up. The students weren't grouped by age – the class included all levels of schooling from grade 8 to grade 12 in the same programme. All the students in Drennie's class were a bit like her. They were full of ideas, keen to experiment with new concepts and, best of all, they were willing to make mistakes and learn from them. Exploring avenues that may turn out to be dead-ends – through a process of trial and error – was encouraged. Drennie's classmates called it "rile and terror". Best of all, there was no rush. Time was allowed for ideas to crystallise and develop into a logical conclusion that could lead to a coherent plan of action.

There were parallel future-proofing classes designed to develop the skills of the more analytically-minded students, and similarly, for the hands-on creatives and those with other abilities. In essence, the classes were teaching the children how to think, based on their innate skills.

To get the class started that day, their teacher had set a challenge that explored product innovation and the types of competition in markets. She read the task out as follows:

> "A few decades ago, document delivery within cities was a thriving business. Motorbikes had a box on the back, and riders nipped speedily in and out of traffic. Some are still

seen today, but nothing like the number of such bikes in the past. Over a period of only a few years during the 1980s, this industry nearly disappeared because of competition. What was the competitive product? You have five minutes to work it out."

The class of twenty students was divided up into groups. There was a group of five, a group of four, two groups of three, and five individuals. They were separated from each other so that nobody could hear what another group was discussing. At each place, they found a piece of paper on which the task was written.

The ever-gregarious Drennie was in the group of five and, not surprisingly, they arrived at the answer first, followed closely by the group of four and the smaller groups. The individuals were the slowest to work it out. The lesson in cooperation was the focus of the discussion that day – that collaboration is one of the key requirements of the twenty-first century. The students saw right away that groups of cooperative individuals would out-compete smaller, less-organised groups or individuals.

It had not been an easy five minutes for Drennie's group. She grabbed the paper and read the challenge out loud to the group. The five innovative students tried to get their ideas heard at the same time, and it took a while to get the thought processes working logically. Drennie eventually took charge and rephrased the question, seeking input from the other four members, starting on her left and working around the circle, one student at a time.

"No! This time I think we should start with Drennie," suggested a seventeen-year-old member of the group, somewhat facetiously. "Well, speak up, Drennie. What ideas do YOU have?"

Drennie was flummoxed. She didn't have any ideas yet, and said so. The others offered their ideas and, bit by bit, they thought each one through, rejecting ideas such as radio-controlled aircraft (which were only controllable in line-of-sight), drones (not invented yet), pigeons (useless for multiple destinations), and flying on broomsticks. Rather than focussing on means of conveyance, they began to think about the outcome – getting information (not necessarily a piece of paper) from one place to another. That's how they arrived at the answer: the commercialisation of the (then) modern fax machine.[22] Before the fax machine was commercialised, a person on a motorbike would usually transport documents between one place and another. Now, those same documents, including drawings, could be sent electronically via a copper telephone line connected to a fax machine. In essence, the same result was achieved using a completely different procedure.

---

22   The anecdote is used courtesy of Ian Clark of Ian Clark Design and Consulting http://clarkdesign.co.za/ .
Ian told me the story while beta testing *Classic 10,* a business strategy course nicknamed *MBA-in-a-Day*. In 2012, usage rights were sold to Team Business LLC in the USA to take *Classic 10* online and deliver it worldwide. Details can be found at: https://www.teambusiness.com/strategy-workshop-mba-in-a-day .

The important conclusion drawn from this exercise was that competition that can 'eat your lunch' doesn't always come from identified competitors. After Drennie's group worked out the solution, they also discussed the fact that, in 2020, the motorbike delivery service industry received a major boost as a result of the COVID-19 pandemic. The delivery of takeaway meals and other goods was in high demand because face-to-face shopping was restricted (or not allowed) during different countries' lockdowns. Online shopping and phone orders grew rapidly, which required a quick activation of small- to medium-sized delivery services, often involving the use of light-duty motorbikes to transport orders to customers. Which then begged the question: What competes with motorbikes now, and what might compete with motorbikes in the future? By the same token, if COVID-19 ceases to be a problem and lockdowns disappear, will the demand for motorbike deliveries continue?

As part of "learning how to think" in their future-proofing class, Drennie's group discussed *how* they had moved from thinking linearly (logically and rationally) and tactically (looking for a quick-fix by asking, simplistically – *what competes with motorbikes?*), to thinking laterally (solving problems creatively) and strategically (planning for the future). Linear, **tactical** thinking had achieved nothing for Drennie's group. It was **strategic**, lateral thinking that led their group to conclude that it was the fax machine that had all but destroyed the intra-city motorbike document delivery industry. In later years, when email was invented, fax machines were used less and less.

HISTORICAL INTEREST BOX - STRATEGY VERSUS TACTICS

For nearly three years during the first half of World War Two, the Allies (the British Empire, USA and others) fought against Axis forces (notably Germany and Italy) in North Africa, mostly in the deserts of Libya and Egypt.[23] The battlefront moved back and forth, east and west, east again, west again, over a stretch of the Sahara Desert spanning thousands of kilometres. The **tactics** involved ground and air forces attacking and defending in a somewhat conventional fashion. The Allies were eventually victorious.

But why were these powerful armies fighting over vast tracts of rock and fly-infested sand and, in the process, incurring a total of nearly eight hundred and sixty thousand casualties?[24] The answer lies in the Axis' **strategy** – gaining access to the Suez Canal and the oil-rich regions of the Middle East. The Allies controlled these regions, and the Axis desperately wanted them.

An easy way to remember the difference between the two terms is to describe one of them: The word *tactics* stems from the words *contact* and *tactile* – relating to touch. In

---

23   David T. Zabecki, *How North Africa Became a Battleground in World War II* (originally published in the March 1997 issue of World War II Magazine), History-Net, https://www.historynet.com/how-north-africa-became-a-battleground-in-world-war-ii.htm .

24   United States Holocaust Memorial Museum, Washington, DC, *Allied Military Operations in North Africa,* https://encyclopedia.ushmm.org/content/en/article/allied-military-operations-in-north-africa .

> other words, tactics refers to quick and immediate actions that need to be taken when *in contact* with the enemy. Strategy involves the setting of longer-term and larger-scale objectives and the requirements for achieving them.

The last ten minutes of the future-proofing class were always spent in silence. All the students made notes for future reference about what they'd learned that day. It was completely private – nobody reviewed or graded their notes.

Drennie had three points. She wrote the following:

1) I am a great team player, but only if I can be the captain. I need to work on that.

2) Groups consisting only of like-minded people can lead to competition rather than collaboration. Leadership in such groups is complicated.

3) Was the make-up of the groups for today's challenge sub-optimal? All twenty members of our class have similar skill sets, which didn't allow for the cross-pollination of approaches. I wonder if we would have got the answer faster if we had had some hands-on fabricators or inventors and other analytically-minded students in our group?

As the class ended, a newcomer asked, "Hey, where'd the teacher go?"

"We switched her off," said Drennie. "She's a hologram from California. Anyway, from next week we don't have to come here unless we want to – we can attend the new 3D virtual school without leaving home. We'll get to dress up as our own individual avatar. I'm sure I'd miss my friends, as I did during the COVID-19 lockdown in 2020-21, so I'll probably attend classes in the flesh while I still can. Perhaps our school will go virtual eventually, and that will become the new normal."

As Drennie headed for Duckie's LactoBactoBuster that afternoon, she was still smarting from the way in which the seventeen-year-old student had challenged her leadership. Later that evening, instead of getting on with her homework, she searched the internet for information about leadership in managing creativity. She found two pertinent quotations:

"It's only by concentrating, sticking to the question, being patient, letting all the parts of my mind come into play, that I arrive at an original idea. By giving my brain a chance to make associations, draw connections, take me by surprise."

William Deresiewicz[25]

---

25   Farnam Street Media Inc., How to Think: The Skill You've Never Been Taught, Farnam Street Media Inc., https://fs.blog/2015/08/how-to-think/ .

and:

> *"An organization's ability to learn, and translate that learning into action rapidly, is the ultimate competitive advantage."*
>
> **Jack Welch,** *former CEO of General Electric*

In a flash, Drennie saw that the first quote related to planning and decision-making, while the second one involved implementation. She juxtaposed those two quotations with the introspection points she'd written down and took a firm decision. While she saw that she was smart enough to be a good leader, she knew that nobody likes a smarty-pants. She also realised that, while teams will always outperform individuals, managing teams is not as easy as it looks.

Drennie thought long and hard about management and leadership. After having mused for long enough, she wrote down her conclusions:

- Professional leadership (where the leader provides direction, process and coordination to their people to achieve an end goal) is more successful than charismatic leadership (where the leader's charm or persuasiveness causes people to follow them), or leadership by demand (where you can order people to perform a particular task or fall in line with set standards, but you can't demand that they see things the way you do).

- Sometimes you have to abandon control and be a supporter or a follower – but only when appropriate. Remember to acknowledge the leadership displayed by others if they're competent.

- Join teams of people whose competence differs from my own.

- Include economics and management in my studies when I finish school.

I woke up smiling at Drennie's last bullet-point, considering how I had struggled to score well in economics previously. There was another reason I was smiling: I knew exactly who the seventeen-year-old character in my dream was – a smart but cocky and assertive boy in a class two years ahead of me who was quite cute, in an interesting sort of way. Not as cute as Claude Treacher, but hey, you can't have everything.

HISTORICAL INTEREST BOX – 'STRETCH GOALS'

Before continuing, re-read the quotation above from the former CEO of General Electric.

In the 1980s, Jack Welch introduced the term "stretch goals" into his management philosophy. The phrase refers to setting goals that are not achievable by "more of the same". These goals are so extreme that innovation is required. Increasing a sales target by a few percent can be achieved by throwing more resources at it. Selling more units of a product can be achieved by hiring additional salespeople, increasing advertising, or offering a quantity discount. That was not what Welch wanted – he was looking for a brand new way of achieving the desired outcome.

In the delivery bike anecdote above, some of the financial pain could have been avoided had the industry participants recognised that they were not in the 'delivery-bike' business but in the 'information-delivery' business. In actual fact, they were in the 'image-delivery' business because text could already be transmitted by telegraph and telex.

I am not suggesting that a bike delivery company should have invented fax technology. What I'm saying is that, once the fax machine began to erode their market, 'stretch goals' (if introduced quickly) would have forced them to think strategically and consider, for example, investing in companies that manufactured fax machines, or setting up a fax business of their own. Whether this would have guaranteed their future survival is anybody's guess. After all, there are no guarantees in business, especially when innovation is involved. Other options may have been more attractive, for example, learning how to dominate sectors of the bike market that required the original document to be delivered. Examples are signed legal documents or engineering drawings that were too large to be faxed.

Bear in mind that, in an industry on the verge of disappearing, simply surviving (even as a smaller, specialist business) is a stretch goal.

This kind of strategic thinking is as appropriate today as it was thirty or forty years ago, but it is not free of risks. For instance, read Andrew Rudin's *"Let's Restore Sanity to Stretch Goals"*.[26]

---

26   Andrew Rudin, Let's Restore Sanity to Stretch Goals, Customer Think, https://customerthink.com/lets-restore-sanity-to-stretch-goals/ .

CHAPTER 11

WHAT'S TO BECOME OF ME?

I thought about my own behaviour and decided to apply the same lessons that Drennie had learned. My life became so much easier when I was no longer trying to control every situation in which I found myself. Oddly, the more I abandoned control, the more people seemed to look to me for leadership. This was leadership by consensus rather than leadership by demand.

My night-time visits to Edel Lawne to witness the daily events in the quaint town yielded additional outcomes for me. Firstly, economics was no longer my most unloved subject — it had been a long while since my teacher had written *"Can do better"* or *"Must try harder"* in my homework book or on my tests. Secondly, while I had never seen myself as a professional leader or an entrepreneur, the more time I spent in Drennie's world, the more the idea appealed to me. What if I were to set up as a competitor to my school's tuckshop? Salty, fatty and sugary treats would be compulsory, and salads would be forbidden. I would have lots of support from all the schoolkids, but I knew I could expect a high level of resistance from the parents and the school's governing body. While the thought of it was amusing, it was not practical. Parents would still control the demand for food by controlling their kids' expenditure, whether using programmed currency or not.

We learned in Chapter 4 that a halfway-decent idea can lead to other – and often better – ideas. I needed a collaborator – the cockier, the better – and I had the perfect person in mind. *Would he work with me*, I wondered? My heart gave a little flutter.

I thought back to the beginning of our story, where Drennie never received any pocket money and value was exchanged for value, and I remembered that Drennie would identify a problem or an opportunity, decide what needed to be done, and then, right away, *she would take action*. Sometimes she didn't even check with her mom first, like when she got her first job operating Duckie's LactoBactoBuster. It suddenly struck me that the answer I was looking for was staring me in the face. Thinking about something achieves little — it is actions that ultimately achieve results.

I thought about the benefits of having a good teacher and how lucky I was to have been able to learn from Drennie's experiences. The fact that I'd had access to both of those advantages put me far ahead of other kids my age — particularly those attending old-fashioned 'chalk-and-talk' schools where future-proofing wasn't included in their curriculum. Only a few fifteen-year-olds have been given such an experiential introduction to the hard facts and fallacies, scams and shams of commerce and economics and the soft skills of strategy, leadership and management.

Since kids like me were in limited supply, I could capitalise on my skills and benefits by making higher profits and earning more money. For someone who once struggled with economics, I suddenly saw a potential career for myself in that field.

While there was still so much for me to learn before I took the gigantic step of applying to a university, in my mind's eye, I saw myself as a highly respected consultant to major tech multinationals, guiding their staff through the concepts of future-proofing. My eyelids began to grow droopy and, soon enough, I was in the strangest dream of all.

The University of Edel Lawne was holding a farewell function for a retiring professor. I almost didn't recognise Drennie. She looked old and grey and must have been about sixty-five. *How did she get to be so old, while I was still fifteen*, I wondered? I guess that can happen in dreams.

But she certainly recognised me. She smiled and handed me the business card she would no longer be using.

Prof. DRENNIE STOCKITT
Dean — Faculty of Economics and
Head of Department — Future-Proofing

Then she smiled an even wider smile and gave me another card — the one that she would be using in future.

Prof. Emerita Dr. DRENNIE STOCKITT
Future-Proofing Consultant
Clients include Google, Amazon, Tesla, SpaceX and Berkshire Hathaway

---

"Jennie," she said, "I'm delighted that economics is no longer causing you so much misery. I know you'll make a success of whatever you turn your mind to. I've taught you all you need to know for the time being, and your knowledge will doubtless supersede mine in the not too distant future. Just take it one step at a time."

Drennie paused and then continued. "Here's one last piece of advice: Look at the companies listed as my clients. In 2021, they were all great companies with great leaders, and they made great profits. But keep an eye on them – not all companies stay great forever. If you need me, you know where to find me. Until then, we have no need to meet again."

I wondered whether I would ever meet Drennie again. I hoped I would, because it would mean that I was wrestling with a problem that I couldn't crack by myself.

And, for me, grappling with an unsolved problem is a good enough reason to get out of bed every morning. I wish the same for you!

GLOSSARY OF TERMS

This glossary of terms provides the meaning of words you may find when reading about matters of economics, commerce and industry. Not all the terms listed appear in this book.

Word or phrase	Meaning
Account (bank)	An arrangement between a bank and an account holder allowing the account holder to deposit and withdraw money.
Account (commerce)	An arrangement between a supplier of goods and/or services and a customer or client allowing value to be provided when required, and for settlement to be made periodically.
Account holder	A person who has entered into an arrangement with a supplier (or bank) for an exchange of value other than an immediate cash payment.

Word or phrase	Meaning
Alter ego	From Latin: "the alternative I" or "the other self". A person's secondary or alternative personality. (Oxford English Dictionary)
Anagram	Words, phrases or names formed by rearranging the letters of other words. Stop, post, pots, spot, tops and opts are examples of anagrams.
Asset	An item of property owned by a person or company regarded as having a value that is available to meet debts. Antonym of a liability.
Bank	A deposit-taking and lending institution.
Bank, central	A country's central bank – the 'banker's bank' – that attempts to control the inflation rate by charging a lower or higher interest rate when commercial banks borrow money for on-lending to their clients. Central banks also control the total money supply in the country and the consequent inflation rate.
Bank, commercial	A bank that provides financial services to persons or companies.

Word or phrase	Meaning
Bank, merchant	A bank that deals mostly with very large transactions, including mergers and acquisitions.
Bank run	Also called a run on the bank. While a bank may be solvent (assets exceed liabilities), it doesn't hold enough cash on hand to satisfy multiple large cash withdrawals at the same time. This starts a rumour that the bank cannot honour its debts. That triggers additional attempts to withdraw cash. The rumour then spreads to other banks and becomes self-fulfilling. See 'Fractional-reserve banking' below.
Barter	The simple swapping of goods or services as a form of trade.
Bearer	One who presents a financial instrument for redemption.
Beneficiary	A person who gains as a result of the actions of others.
Bitcoin	The oldest and most widely used cryptocurrency.

Word or phrase	Meaning
Blockchain	A system of integrated electronic ledgers dispersed throughout the world. Blockchain is the underlying technology that controls the creation of new crypto values and records every transaction. The integration of blockchain technology with the Internet of things (IoT) holds the potential to (disruptively) re-engineer traditional commerce and industry.
Cash	Money in the form of coins or notes – as distinct from cheques, money orders, EFTs, cryptocurrencies (and so on) that can also be used to purchase goods and services and to pay debts.
Cheque, Check	A financial instrument by which an account holder at a bank instructs the bank to pay defined monies to a recipient (beneficiary). With the advent of mobile and internet banking, many banks are phasing out cheques (or have already done so).

Word or phrase	Meaning
Cheshire Cat's grin	In the fantasy tale "Alice in Wonderland", the Cheshire Cat could disappear, leaving only his grin behind.
Chit	An informal note acknowledging a debt, such as for food or drink.
Code base, codebase	A codebase is the complete body of source code for a given software program or application. Source code is the version of a program that a programmer writes and saves as a file. Elaboration can be found at https://whatis.techtarget.com/definition/codebase-code-base
Commodity	A product that can be bought and sold.
Credit (In credit)	An account in which funds are held in trust by a deposit-taking institution and owed to the account holder (depositor). Opposite of 'in debit'.
Credit (On credit)	The ability of a customer to obtain goods or services before payment, based on the seller's belief that payment will be made in the future.

Word or phrase	Meaning
Creditor	A person or company to whom money is owed. Originally derived from the Latin *'credo'*, meaning *'I believe'*. Creditors *believe* that debts will be repaid. Antonym of debtor.
Crypto	Contraction of cryptocurrency.
Cryptocurrency	A medium of exchange based on the exchange and recordal of digital information. Most cryptocurrencies use blockchain technology. Cryptography is used to secure the transactions and control the creation of additional currency. The origin of every crypto transaction can be traced back to its creation. To date, the values of cryptocurrencies have been skewed by hoarding in the hope that the value of the crypto (in fiat currency after conversion) will increase. In other words, cryptos have been viewed more as investments than as mediums of exchange. This volatility has eroded trust in the cryptos' primary purpose – the exchange of value.

Word or phrase	Meaning
Currency	A money system, usually referring to that which is used in a particular country.
Debit (In debit)	A facility in which the account holder owes money (in excess of what was agreed at any time) to the deposit-taking institution. If the account administrator is a deposit-taking institution such as a bank, the term is synonymous with 'in overdraft'. The opposite of 'in credit'.
Debit order	An account holder authorises the bank to release funds against a demand from a third party.
Debtor	A person or business that owes something – usually money. From the Latin *debitum*. Antonym of creditor.
Defray	Bear, pay or settle (costs, expenses, debts, etc.).
Deposit-taking institution	An organisation – typically, a bank – that accepts funds and holds them in trust on behalf of its account holders. In most countries, operating this type of enterprise requires a government licence.

Word or phrase	Meaning
Deservedness	A state or quality of having been justly earned.
Draft ('Bank draft')	A bank draft is also called a 'banker's bill'. It is an instruction from one bank to another for the purpose of paying money.
Draft ('First draft')	A first or preliminary form of a document, subject to revision. Not to be confused with 'bank draft'.
Edel Lawne	The name of the town in our story, an anagram of 'All We Need'.
Efficiency	A measure of the valuable outputs compared to the inputs. Inputs may include time, effort, skill, money, labour and raw materials, while outputs could be finished work or products.
EFT (Electronic Funds Transfer)	Using digital technology to (for example) provide a payment instruction to a bank.
Emerita	Prof. Emeritus (masculine) and Prof. Emerita (feminine) are honorary titles bestowed upon retired academics.

Word or phrase	Meaning
Facility (finance)	An arrangement whereby a financial institution or supplier extends a service (such as an overdraft or deferred payment) to a client.
Fiat money	From the Latin *'Let it be done'*. A currency that is declared to have value and be legal tender by government decree, but is not exchangeable against any physical commodity held as collateral by the government or its agent (typically the central bank).
Financial instrument	A negotiable instrument.
Fractional-reserve banking	The principle by which commercial banks can only lend borrowers a portion of the cash received from its depositors. The balance (usually 10%) must be held in reserve.
Fungible	Exchangeable. Capable of being converted from one form of value to another.

Word or phrase	Meaning
GDP	Gross Domestic Product: the value of all the goods and services produced within a country. It can be reported as "nominal" GDP (not taking inflation into account). Alternatively, it can be reported as 'constant-price', 'inflation-corrected', or 'constant dollar' GDP (after allowing for inflation.) It is usually reported annually or quarterly, within a year. The annual or quarterly change is normally reported as a percentage, rather than the actual value of GDP.
Inflation	The rate at which the value of a currency decreases as time goes by. Inflation causes an increase in the price of all goods and services produced in a country.
Inflation, Cost-push	Inflation caused by an increase in the cost of production, typically raw materials and wages. In order to maintain financial viability, suppliers must raise the prices of their wares.

Word or phrase	Meaning
Inflation, Demand-pull	Inflation caused by an over-supply of money – often the result of low interest rates or the uncontrolled printing of banknotes. When interest rates are low, money is cheap to borrow, so people borrow to purchase goods which would normally be too expensive. Prices increase because the demand for goods is artificially or unrealistically high.
Inflation, imported	A form of cost-push inflation resulting from an increase in the price of imported goods and services caused by a depreciation in the importing currency's value against that of the supply currency.
Interest	Money paid to a lender in return for the use of money that has been borrowed.
IoT (Internet of things)	Electro-mechanical devices that communicate with each other and achieve results without human intervention.
Inventory	Stock. A quantity of goods held and ready to be supplied.

Word or phrase	Meaning
IOU	"I owe you" – an informal note recording a promise to pay.
Legal tender	Banknotes or coins that the seller or creditor is obliged to accept in payment for goods or settlement of a debt.
Liability	Something for which a person or business is responsible, especially an amount of money owed. Antonym of Asset.
Make money	To create wealth – a consequence of creating or adding value.
Medium of exchange	An intermediate indication of value that simplifies trade, including coins, banknotes and negotiable documents.
Money	Coins and banknotes (also see 'Near money').
Money supply	The entire stock of currency and other instruments in a country's economy at any given time, such as coins, notes and balances held in deposit accounts.
Near money	Assets that can be readily converted into cash, such as a negotiable instrument.

Word or phrase	Meaning
Negotiable Instrument	A document that can be traded (see 'Trade').
Overdraft	A facility provided by a deposit-taking institution that allows the account holder to withdraw funds in excess of what has been deposited. The account will hold a negative balance, and the account holder will owe money to the institution.
Overdraft (unauthorised)	A situation where the account holder has withdrawn – or attempted to withdraw – funds that exceed the agreed limit.
Overdrawn	When the funds that are withdrawn from an account exceed the funds on deposit.

Word or phrase	Meaning
Paper. Also 'Commercial Paper'	A written instrument or document – such as a cheque (check), bank draft, promissory note, or certificate of deposit that manifests the pledge or duty of one individual or business to pay money to another. One of the most significant aspects of commercial paper is that it is negotiable – in other words, it can be freely transferred from one party to another, either through endorsement or delivery. The terms *commercial paper* and *negotiable instrument* can be used interchangeably.
Promissory Note	A formal signed document containing a promise to pay a stated sum to a specified person or bearer on a specified date or on-demand.
Redeem, redemption	The fulfilment of the requirements contained in a financial instrument.
Retail	Selling in moderate and small quantities to end-users, cf. Wholesale.

GLOSSARY OF TERMS | 145

Word or phrase	Meaning
Settlement	The provision of value to defray debts, expenses, etc.
Specie	Cash in the form of coins, as distinct from banknotes.
Superteacher	In British education, an informal name for an advanced skills teacher (Collins English Dictionary).
Tick (on tick)	On credit.
Token	Something that provides a tangible representation of value or rights.
Trade	The voluntary exchange of value in the form of goods, services or documentation – including money.
Treasury	The 'nation's bank account' held at the central bank (see 'Bank, central').
Wholesale	Selling in large quantities to resellers, cf. Retail.

TABLE OF FIGURES

Figure No.	Reference
Figure i	Olaus Magnus, *History of the Nordic Peoples (from 1555) - Illustrations with comments, Book 4 Ch. 5. On Trade Without Using Money*, Copyright-free Scandinavian Archive Prints in High Quality and High Resolution Image source: http://www.avrosys.nu/prints/prints27-olausmagnus.htm Copyright authorisation: Kind permission of image owner, Lars Henriksson
Figure ii	Dane Kurth, *Lydian Lion* Numismatic database Wildwinds Co. Ltd. ex *CNG Mail bid sale 58 (2001)* Image source: http://www.wildwinds.com/coins/greece/lydia/kings/kroisos/SNGCop_455.jpg Copyright authorisation: Kind permission of database curator Kurth, D.

Figure No.	Reference
Figure iii	H. Zell, *Dirty Cowry; Length 2.9 cm; Originating from Hersonissos, Crete, Greece; Shell of own collection, therefore not geocoded. Dorsal, lateral (right side), ventral, back, and front view*
	By H. Zell, Own work: https://commons.wikimedia.org/wiki/User:Llez/Shells_by_H._Zell
	Image source: https://commons.wikimedia.org/w/index.php?title=File:Erosaria_spurca_spurca_01.JPG&oldid=505918517
	Copyright authorisation: CC BY-SA 3.0, via Wikimedia Commons
Figure iv	Bill Maurer, *Ghana 1 cedi coin with cowrie shell image*
	Institute for Money, Technology and Financial Inclusion
	Image source: https://www.flickr.com/photos/imtfi/5867792575/
	Copyright authorisation: Creative Commons Attribution Share Alike 2.0 Generic. Free Cultural Works

Figure No.	Reference
Figure v	Gift of Miss Frances S. Reilly: Coll. of her father John Reilly Jr, *Bone cowrie, China, 500 BC - 221 BC. Obverse: shell teeth imitation* American Numismatic Society Image source: http://numismatics.org/collection/1937.179.4191 Copyright authorisation: Public Domain
Figure vi	Dane Kurth, *Aureus* Numismatic database Wildwinds Co. Ltd ex Gemini IV Auction (2008) Image source: http://www.wildwinds.com/coins/sear5/s1396.html Copyright authorisation: Kind permission of database curator Kurth, D.

Figure No.	Reference
Figure vii	Dane Kurth, *Clipped Solidus* Numismatic database Wildwinds Co. Ltd ex Roma Numismatics Ltd E-Sale 71, Lot 1335, May 2020 Image source: http://wildwinds.com/coins/ric/jovian/_antioch_RIC_223_A.jpg Copyright authorisation: Kind permission of database curator Kurth, D.
Figure viii	Amelia Spink, *Silver and gold round coins photo Free coin image on Unsplash* Unsplash Photos for everyone Image source: https://unsplash.com/photos/xX7rb_8EkJk Copyright authorisation: Free coin image on Unsplash

Figure No.	Reference
Figure ix	Newman Numismatic Portal at Washington University in St. Louis, *$1 1928D Silver Certificate* Image source: https://nnp.wustl.edu/library/ImageDetail/582150 Copyright authorisation: Compliant with regulations at https://www.treasury.gov/services/Pages/Regulations-for-Reproducing-US-Currency-Images.aspx
Figure x	Newman Numismatic Portal at Washington University in St. Louis, *$10 1907 Gold Certificate* Image source: https://nnp.wustl.edu/library/ImageDetail/581856 Copyright authorisation: Compliant with regulations at https://www.treasury.gov/services/Pages/Regulations-for-Reproducing-US-Currency-Images.aspx

Figure No.	Reference
Figure xi	Newman Numismatic Portal at Washington University in St. Louis, *$5 1914 Federal Reserve Note* Image source: https://nnp.wustl.edu/library/ImageDetail/581698 Copyright authorisation: Compliant with regulations at https://www.treasury.gov/services/Pages/Regulations-for-Reproducing-US-Currency-Images.aspx
Figure xii	Privately owned: NORLU, https://de.wikipedia.org/wiki/Benutzer:NORLU, *Voucher worth fifty trillion marks. The highest value given by the cities of Eschweiler and Stolberg (Issued November 11, 1923)* Image source: https://commons.wikimedia.org/wiki/File:50_Billionen_Mark_Stolberg_Eschweiler_001.jpg Copyright authorisation: Public domain

Figure No.	Reference
Figure xiii	Reserve Bank of Zimbabwe, *One hundred trillion Zimbabwe dollar note* Image source: https://en.wikipedia.org/wiki/File:Zimbabwe_$100_trillion_2009_Obverse.jpg Copyright authorisation: Public domain according to section 50 of the Copyright Act [Chapter 26:1] of Zimbabwe

About the Author:

John Hofmeyr's debut novella *From Barter to Bitcoin* follows unpublished works that include two short ghost stories, a Christmas pageant narrated from the donkey's viewpoint, a hymn, some benedicites, and a few poems.

John has retired from twenty-five years in the industrial chemistry and process engineering industries and ten in the business of electricity and water distribution hardware. For the past fifteen years, he has been involved in biochar – using charcoal to improve soil fertility (and other applications) – while simultaneously sequestering atmospheric carbon as a Negative Emission Technology; John's little contribution to saving the world. Some of his techno-commercial work is published on the Researchgate web site.

John drank freely from the fountains of knowledge at the University of Hard Knocks. His industrial career gave free rein to try out novel products and procedures and the freedom to make mistakes and learn from them.

He solved a challenging variety of techno-commercial problems that led to profitable businesses. Perhaps that's the mould in which the protagonist in *From Barter to Bitcoin* is cast.

Problem-solving opened many doors for John. Business invitations have taken him to diverse destinations, including the US Bureau of Mines, the electricity and water utilities in Rwanda, Uganda, Jordan and Palestine, Washington DC (to present a paper on the prepaid metering of water at the World Bank), and London for South Africa Day at the Royal Society. He was also invited by Iraqi electricity utilities to lecture on prepaid electricity coupled with load management. (The no-fly restrictions required 1100 miles of taxi rides from Amman to Baghdad and back again.) As a memento, he still has his quaint Iraqi visa that makes no reference to his surname. The travels were seldom fun but inevitably instructive.

John lives quietly in Johannesburg, South Africa. He is a Life Member of the South African Chemical Institute and has Professional Membership of the International Biochar Initiative.

www.ingramcontent.com/pod-product-compliance
Lightning Source LLC
Chambersburg PA
CBHW062049290426
44109CB00027B/2774